COOK'S KITCHEN

Beautiful Bakes

igloobooks

Published in 2014
by Igloo Books Ltd
Cottage Farm
Sywell
NN6 0BJ
www.igloobooks.com

The measurements used are approximate.

Food photography and recipe development: PhotoCuisine UK

OCE001 0714
2 4 6 8 10 9 7 5 3 1
ISBN 978-1-78343-527-2

Printed and manufactured in China

Contents

Breads

Wholemeal Basil Bread

MAKES 1 LOAF

PREPARATION TIME 2 HOURS 30 MINUTES

COOKING TIME 35–40 MINUTES

INGREDIENTS

200 g / 7 oz / 1 ⅓ cups strong white bread flour, plus extra for dusting
200 g / 7 oz / 1 ⅓ cups stoneground wholemeal flour
½ tsp easy-blend dried yeast
1 tbsp caster (superfine) sugar
1 tsp fine sea salt
a small bunch of basil, chopped
3 tbsp olive oil

METHOD

- Mix together the flours, yeast, sugar, salt and basil. Stir in the oil into 280 ml / 9 fl. oz / 1 cup warm water, then mix with the dry ingredients.
- Knead the mixture on a lightly oiled surface for 10 minutes or until smooth and elastic. Leave the dough to rest in an oiled bowl for 1–2 hours or until doubled in size.
- Roll the dough with your hands into a fat sausage, then turn it 90° and roll it tightly the other way. Tuck the ends under and transfer the dough to a square or rectangular loaf tin, keeping the seam underneath. Cover the tin loosely with oiled cling film and leave to prove somewhere warm for 45 minutes.
- Preheat the oven to 220°C (200°C fan) / 430F / gas 7.
- Transfer the tin to the top shelf of the oven, then close the door. Bake for 35–40 minutes or until the loaf sounds hollow when you tap it underneath. Transfer the bread to a wire rack and leave to cool completely before slicing.

Sesame Rolls

MAKES 12

PREPARATION TIME 2 HOURS 30 MINUTES

COOKING TIME 15 MINUTES

INGREDIENTS

400 g / 14 oz / 2 ⅔ cups strong white bread flour, plus extra for dusting
½ tsp easy-blend dried yeast
1 tbsp caster (superfine) sugar
1 tsp fine sea salt
1 tbsp sesame oil
3 tbsp sesame seeds

METHOD

- Mix together the flour, yeast, sugar and salt. Stir the oil into 280 ml / 9 fl. oz / 1 cup of warm water then stir it into the dry ingredients.
- Knead the mixture on a lightly oiled surface for 10 minutes or until smooth and elastic. Leave the dough to rest, covered with oiled cling film, for 1–2 hours or until doubled in size.
- Shape the dough into 12 rolls and transfer to a greased baking tray, then cover with oiled cling film and leave to prove for 1 hour or until doubled in size.
- Preheat the oven to 220°C (200°C fan) / 425F / gas 7.
- Slash a cross into the top of each roll with a sharp knife and sprinkle with sesame seeds. Transfer the tray to the top shelf of the oven then close the door.
- Bake for 15 minutes or until the rolls sound hollow when you tap them underneath. Transfer to a wire rack and leave to cool completely before serving.

Rice Bread

MAKES 1 LOAF

PREPARATION TIME 2 HOURS 30 MINUTES

COOKING TIME 35–40 MINUTES

INGREDIENTS

300 g / 10 ½ oz / 2 cups strong white bread flour, plus extra for dusting
½ tsp easy-blend dried yeast
1 tbsp caster (superfine) sugar
1 tsp fine sea salt
300 g / 10 ½ oz / 1 ¾ cups cooked white rice, cooled
1 tbsp olive oil

METHOD

- Mix together the flour, yeast, sugar, and salt. Stir the rice and oil into 280 ml / 9 fl. oz / 1 cup of warm water and mix with the dry ingredients.
- Knead the dough on a lightly oiled surface for 10 minutes or until smooth and elastic. Leave the dough to rest, covered with oiled cling film, for 1–2 hours or until doubled in size.
- Roll the dough into a fat sausage. Turn it 90° and roll it tightly the other way then tuck the ends under and transfer the dough to a greased loaf tin, keeping the seam underneath.
- Cover the tin and leave to prove for 1 hour or until doubled in size.
- Meanwhile, preheat the oven to 220°C (200°C fan) / 430F / gas 7.
- Bake for 35–40 minutes or until the loaf sounds hollow when you tap it underneath. Transfer the bread to a wire rack and leave to cool completely before slicing.

Yoghurt Bread

MAKES 2 LOAVES
PREPARATION TIME 2 HOURS 30 MINUTES
COOKING TIME 30 MINUTES

INGREDIENTS

300 g / 10 ½ oz / 2 cups strong white bread flour, plus extra for dusting
½ tsp easy-blend dried yeast
1 tbsp caster (superfine) sugar
1 tsp fine sea salt
300 ml / 10 ½ fl. oz / 1 ¼ cups natural yoghurt, plus extra for brushing

METHOD

- Mix together the flour, yeast, sugar, and salt, then stir in the yoghurt.
- Knead the dough on a lightly oiled surface for 10 minutes or until smooth and elastic. Leave the dough to rest, covered with oiled cling film, for 1–2 hours or until doubled in size.
- Divide the dough in half and shape each piece into a square loaf. Transfer to a greased baking tray, cover with oiled cling film and leave to prove for 1 hour or until doubled in size.
- Meanwhile, preheat the oven to 220°C (200°C fan) / 430F / gas 7.
- Brush the top of the loaves with yoghurt or leave them plain. Bake for 30 minutes or until the loaves sound hollow when you tap them underneath. Transfer to a wire rack and leave to cool completely.

Granary and Rye Batons

MAKES 8

PREPARATION TIME 2 HOURS 30 MINUTES

COOKING TIME 20 MINUTES

INGREDIENTS

200 g / 7 oz / 1 ⅓ cups malted granary flour
200 g / 7 oz / 1 ⅓ cups rye flour
1 tsp easy-blend dried yeast
2 tbsp caster (superfine) sugar
2 tbsp poppy seeds
1 tsp fine sea salt
1 tbsp olive oil

METHOD

- Mix together the flours, yeast, sugar, poppy seeds and salt. Stir the oil into 280 ml / 9 fl. oz / 1 cup of warm water then stir it into the dry ingredients.
- Knead the mixture on a lightly oiled surface with your hands for 10 minutes or until smooth and elastic. Leave the dough to rest in a lightly oiled bowl, covered with oiled cling film, for 1–2 hours or until doubled in size.
- Knead it for 2 more minutes then divide it into 8 pieces and shape into slender batons. Transfer the batons to a greased baking tray and cover with oiled cling film. Leave to prove for 1 hour or until doubled in size.
- Meanwhile, preheat the oven to 220°C (200°C fan) / 425F / gas 7.
- Transfer the tray to the top shelf of the oven. Bake for 20 minutes or until the batons sound hollow when you tap them underneath. Transfer to a wire rack and leave to cool completely.

Cranberry and Flaked Almond Loaf

SERVES 8

PREPARATION TIME 15 MINUTES

COOKING TIME 55 MINUTES

INGREDIENTS

225 g / 8 oz self / 1 ½ cups self-raising flour
100 g / 3 ½ oz / ½ cup butter, cubed
85 g / 3 oz / ⅓ cup caster (superfine) sugar
150 g / 5 ½ oz / ¾ cup dried cranberries
75 g / 2 ½ oz / 1 cup flaked (slivered) almonds
1 large egg
75 ml / 2 ½ fl. oz / ⅓ cup whole milk

METHOD

- Preheat the oven to 180°C (160°C fan) / 355F / gas 4 and line a loaf tin with non-stick baking paper.
- Sieve the flour into a mixing bowl and rub in the butter until it resembles fine breadcrumbs then stir in the sugar, cranberries and almonds.
- Lightly beat the egg with the milk and stir it into the dry ingredients until just combined.
- Scrape the mixture into the loaf tin and bake for 55 minutes or until a skewer inserted into the centre comes out clean.
- Transfer the cake to a wire rack and leave to cool completely.

White Bread Rolls

MAKES 12

PREPARATION TIME 2 HOURS 30 MINUTES

COOKING TIME 15 MINUTES

INGREDIENTS

400 g / 14 oz / 2 ⅔ cups strong white bread flour, plus extra for dusting
½ tsp easy-blend dried yeast
1 tbsp caster (superfine) sugar
1 tsp fine sea salt
1 tbsp olive oil

METHOD

- Mix together the flour, yeast, sugar and salt. Stir the oil into 280 ml / 9 fl. oz / 1 cup of warm water then stir it into the dry ingredients.
- Knead the mixture on a lightly oiled surface for 10 minutes or until smooth and elastic. Leave the dough to rest, covered with oiled cling film, for 1–2 hours or until doubled in size.
- Shape the dough into 12 rolls and transfer to a greased baking tray, then cover with oiled cling film and leave to prove for 1 hour or until doubled in size.
- Preheat the oven to 220°C (200°C fan) / 425F / gas 7.
- Dust the rolls with a little flour and slash a cross into the top of each one with a sharp knife. Transfer the tray to the top shelf of the oven, then close the door.
- Bake for 15 minutes or until the rolls sound hollow when you tap them underneath. Transfer to a wire rack and leave to cool completely before serving.

Onion Focaccia

MAKES 1

PREPARATION TIME 2 HOURS 30 MINUTES

COOKING TIME 25 MINUTES

INGREDIENTS

300 g / 10 ½ oz / 2 cups strong white bread flour
½ tsp easy-blend dried yeast
1 tsp fine sea salt
2 tbsp olive oil
1 onion, quartered and thinly sliced
1 tbsp thyme leaves
50 ml / 1 ¾ fl. oz / ¼ cup olive oil
50 ml / 1 ¾ fl. oz /¼ cup warm water
½ tsp fine sea salt

METHOD

- Mix together the flour, yeast and salt. Stir the oil into 280 ml / 9 fl. oz / 1 cup of warm water then stir it into the dry ingredients.
- Knead the mixture on a lightly oiled surface for 10 minutes or until smooth and elastic. Leave the dough to rest, covered with oiled cling film, for 1–2 hours or until doubled in size.
- Oil a rectangular cake tin then stretch out the dough to cover the base. Cover the focaccia with oiled cling film and leave to prove for 1 hour or until doubled in size.
- Preheat the oven to 220°C (200°C fan) / 430F / gas 7.
- Sprinkle the onion and thyme over the top of the focaccia and press down lightly. Put the oil, water and salt in a jam jar and shake well to emulsify. Pour it all over the dough.
- Transfer the tin to the top shelf of the oven. Bake for 25 minutes or until the top is golden and the base is cooked through. Leave to cool on a wire rack before cutting into squares.

Sweetcorn Rolls

MAKES 16

PREPARATION TIME 2 HOURS 30 MINUTES

COOKING TIME 15 MINUTES

INGREDIENTS

400 g / 14 oz / 2 ⅔ cups strong white bread flour, plus extra for dusting
½ tsp easy-blend dried yeast
1 tbsp caster (superfine) sugar
1 tsp fine sea salt
1 tbsp olive oil
100 g / 3 ½ oz / ½ cup canned sweetcorn, drained

METHOD

- Mix together the flour, yeast, sugar and salt. Stir the oil and sweetcorn into 280 ml / 9 fl. oz / 1 cup of warm water then stir it into the dry ingredients.
- Knead the mixture on a lightly oiled surface for 10 minutes or until smooth and elastic. Leave the dough to rest in a lightly oiled bowl, covered with oiled cling film, for 1–2 hours or until doubled in size.
- Knead the dough for 2 more minutes then split it into 16 even pieces and shape into rolls. Transfer the rolls to a greased baking tray and cover with oiled cling film. Leave to prove for 1 hour or until doubled in size.
- Meanwhile, preheat the oven to 220°C (200°C fan) / 425F / gas 7.
- Transfer the tray to the top shelf of the oven, then close the door. Bake for 15 minutes or until the rolls sound hollow when you tap them underneath. Transfer to a wire rack and leave to cool completely.

Black Olive and Feta Bread

MAKES 1 LOAF

PREPARATION TIME 2 HOURS 30 MINUTES

COOKING TIME 35–40 MINUTES

INGREDIENTS

300 g / 10 ½ oz / 2 cups strong white bread flour, plus extra for dusting
100 g / 3 ½ oz / ⅔ cup stoneground wholemeal flour
½ tsp easy-blend dried yeast
1 tbsp caster (superfine) sugar
1 tsp fine sea salt
100 g / 3 ½ oz / ½ cup feta, cubed
100 g / 3 ½ oz / ½ cup black olives, pitted and sliced

METHOD

- Mix together the flours, yeast, sugar and salt. Stir the feta and olives into 280 ml / 9 fl. oz / 1 cup of warm water and stir into the dry ingredients.
- Knead the mixture on a lightly oiled surface for 10 minutes or until the dough is smooth and elastic. Leave the dough to rest in a lightly oiled bowl, covered with oiled cling film, for 1–2 hours or until doubled in size.
- Knead the dough for 2 more minutes then roll it into a fat sausage. Turn it 90° and roll it tightly the other way then tuck the ends under and transfer the dough to the tin, keeping the seam underneath.
- Cover the tin with oiled cling film and leave to prove for 45 minutes.
- Preheat the oven to 220°C (200°C fan) / 430F / gas 7.
- Transfer the tin to the top shelf of the oven, close the door. Bake for 35–40 minutes or until the underneath sounds hollow when tapped. Leave to cool completely on a wire rack before slicing.

Crusty Lemon Rolls

MAKES 4

PREPARATION TIME 2 HOURS 30 MINUTES

COOKING TIME 20 MINUTES

INGREDIENTS

400 g / 14 oz / 2 ⅔ cups strong white bread flour, plus extra for dusting
½ tsp easy-blend dried yeast
1 tbsp caster (superfine) sugar
1 tsp fine sea salt
1 lemon, juiced and zest finely grated
1 tbsp olive oil

METHOD

- Mix together the flour, yeast, sugar, salt and lemon zest. Stir the oil and lemon juice into 250 ml / 9 fl. oz / 1 cup of warm water then stir it into the dry ingredients.
- Knead the mixture on a lightly oiled surface for 10 minutes or until smooth and elastic. Leave the dough to rest, covered with oiled cling film, for 1–2 hours or until doubled in size.
- Shape the dough into 4 long rolls and transfer to a greased baking tray, then cover with oiled cling film and leave to prove for 1 hour or until doubled in size.
- Preheat the oven to 220°C (200°C fan) / 425F / gas 7.
- Slash the top of each roll diagonally with a sharp knife. Transfer the tray to the top shelf of the oven, then close the door.
- Bake for 20 minutes or until the rolls sound hollow when you tap them underneath. Transfer to a wire rack and leave to cool completely before serving.

Floured Cob

MAKES 1

PREPARATION TIME 2 HOURS 30 MINUTES

COOKING TIME 40 MINUTES

INGREDIENTS

400 g / 14 oz / 2 ⅔ cups strong white bread flour, plus extra for dusting
½ tsp easy-blend dried yeast
1 tbsp caster (superfine) sugar
1 tsp fine sea salt
1 tbsp olive oil

METHOD

- Mix together the flour, yeast, sugar and salt. Stir the oil into 280 ml / 9 fl. oz / 1 cup of warm water then stir it into the dry ingredients.
- Knead the mixture on a lightly oiled surface for 10 minutes or until smooth and elastic. Leave the dough to rest, covered with oiled cling film, for 1–2 hours or until doubled in size.
- Shape the dough into a round cob loaf and transfer to a greased baking tray, then cover with oiled cling film and leave to prove for 1 hour or until doubled in size.
- Preheat the oven to 220°C (200°C fan) / 425F / gas 7.
- Dust the loaf with flour. Transfer the tray to the top shelf of the oven, then close the door. Bake for 40 minutes or until the loaf sounds hollow when you tap it underneath. Transfer to a wire rack and leave to cool completely before serving.

Grape and Rosemary Focaccia

MAKES 1

PREPARATION TIME 2 HOURS 30 MINUTES

COOKING TIME 25 MINUTES

INGREDIENTS

300 g / 10 ½ oz / 2 cups strong white bread flour
½ tsp easy-blend dried yeast
1 tsp fine sea salt
2 tbsp olive oil

TO FINISH

75 g / 2 ½ oz / ½ cup seedless red grapes
1 tbsp rosemary
50 ml / 1 ¾ fl. oz / ¼ cup olive oil
50 ml / 1 ¾ fl. oz / ¼ cup warm water
½ tsp sea salt crystals

METHOD

- Mix together the flour, yeast and salt. Stir the oil into 280 ml / 9 fl. oz / 1 cup of warm water then stir it into the dry ingredients.
- Knead the mixture on a lightly oiled surface for 10 minutes or until smooth and elastic. Leave the dough to rest, covered with oiled cling film, for 1–2 hours or until doubled in size.
- Oil a baking sheet then roll or stretch out the dough to a large oval. Place on the tray, cover with oiled cling film and leave to prove for 1 hour or until doubled in size.
- Preheat the oven to 220°C (200°C fan) / 430F / gas 7.
- Sprinkle the grapes and rosemary over the top of the focaccia and press down lightly. Put the oil, water and salt in a jam jar and shake well to emulsify. Pour it all over the dough.
- Transfer the tin to the top shelf of the oven, then close the door. Bake for 25 minutes or until the top is golden and the base is cooked through. Leave to cool on a wire rack before cutting into squares.

Rosemary Focaccia

MAKES 1

PREPARATION TIME 2 HOURS 30 MINUTES

COOKING TIME 25 MINUTES

INGREDIENTS

300 g / 10 ½ oz / 2 cups strong white bread flour
½ tsp easy-blend dried yeast
1 tsp fine sea salt
2 tbsp olive oil

TO FINISH

50 ml / 1 ¾ fl. oz / ¼ cup olive oil
50 ml / 1 ¾ fl. oz / ¼ cup warm water
½ tsp fine sea salt
1 tsp dried rosemary

METHOD

- Mix together the flour, yeast and salt. Stir the oil into 280 ml / 9 fl. oz / 1 cup of warm water then stir it into the dry ingredients.
- Knead the mixture on a lightly oiled surface for 10 minutes or until smooth and elastic.
- Leave the dough to rest, covered with oiled cling film, for 1–2 hours or until doubled in size.
- Oil a baking sheet then roll or stretch out the dough to a large oval. Place on the tray.
- Cover the focaccia with oiled cling film and leave to prove for 1 hour or until doubled in size.
- Preheat the oven to 220°C (200°C fan) / 430F / gas 7.
- Put the oil, water and salt in a jam jar and shake well to emulsify. Pour it all over the dough then sprinkle with the rosemary. Transfer the tin to the top shelf of the oven.
- Bake for 25 minutes, then leave to cool on a wire rack before cutting into squares.

Tear and share Rolls

MAKES 9

PREPARATION TIME 2 HOURS 30 MINUTES

COOKING TIME 25 MINUTES

INGREDIENTS

400 g / 14 oz / 2 ⅔ cups strong white bread flour, plus extra for dusting
½ tsp easy-blend dried yeast
1 tbsp caster (superfine) sugar
1 tsp fine sea salt
1 tbsp olive oil

METHOD

- Mix together the flour, yeast, sugar and salt. Stir the oil into 280 ml / 9 fl. oz / 1 cup of warm water then stir it into the dry ingredients.
- Knead the mixture on a lightly oiled surface for 10 minutes or until smooth and elastic. Leave the dough to rest, covered with oiled cling film, for 1–2 hours or until doubled in size.
- Shape the dough into 9 rolls and transfer to a greased cast iron sauté pan or large round cake tin. Cover with oiled cling film and leave to prove for 1 hour or until doubled in size and the rolls are all touching.
- Preheat the oven to 220°C (200°C fan) / 425F / gas 7.
- Slash a cross into the top of each roll with a sharp knife. Transfer the tray to the top shelf of the oven, then close the door.
- Bake for 25 minutes or until the rolls sound hollow when you tap them underneath. Transfer to a wire rack and leave to cool completely before serving.

Cinnamon and Raisin Bread

MAKES 1 LOAF

PREPARATION TIME 2 HOURS 30 MINUTES

COOKING TIME 35–40 MINUTES

INGREDIENTS

400 g / 14 oz / 2 ⅔ cups strong white bread flour, plus extra for dusting
½ tsp easy-blend dried yeast
1 tbsp caster (superfine) sugar
1 tsp ground cinnamon
1 tsp fine sea salt
100 g / 3 ½ oz / ½ cup raisins
1 tbsp butter, melted
1 egg, beaten

METHOD

- Mix together the flour, yeast, sugar, cinnamon, salt and raisins. Stir the butter into 280 ml / 9 fl. oz / 1 cup of warm water. Stir the liquid into the dry ingredients then knead on a lightly oiled surface for 10 minutes or until the dough is smooth and elastic.
- Leave the dough to rest, covered with oiled cling film, for 1–2 hours or until doubled in size.
- Knead the dough for 2 more minutes, then shape it into a long loaf. Transfer the dough to a greased loaf tin and cover again with oiled cling film. Leave to prove for 1 hour or until doubled in size.
- Meanwhile, preheat the oven to 220°C (200°C fan) / 425F / gas 7.
- When the dough has risen, brush the top with beaten egg and score a diamond pattern across the top. Transfer the tin to the top shelf of the oven close the door. Bake for 35–40 minutes or until the loaf is golden and sounds hollow when tapped.

Seed-topped Square Rolls

MAKES 9 ROLLS

PREPARATION TIME 2 HOURS 30 MINUTES

COOKING TIME 12 MINUTES

INGREDIENTS

400 g / 14 oz / 2 ⅔ cups strong white bread flour, plus extra for dusting
½ tsp easy-blend dried yeast
1 tbsp caster (superfine) sugar
1 tsp fine sea salt
2 tbsp olive oil
2 tbsp milk
sesame seeds, poppy seeds and linseeds for sprinkling

METHOD

- Mix together the flour, yeast, sugar and salt. Stir the oil into 280 ml / 9 fl. oz / 1 cup of warm water then stir the liquid into the dry ingredients.
- Knead the mixture on a lightly oiled surface for 10 minutes or until smooth and elastic. Leave the dough to rest, covered with oiled cling film, for 1–2 hours or until doubled in size.
- Roll out the dough into a square, then cut it into 9 rolls and transfer to a greased baking tray. Cover the rolls with oiled cling film and leave to prove for 1 hour or until doubled in size.
- Preheat the oven to 220°C (200°C fan) / 430F / gas 7.
- Brush the rolls with milk and sprinkle the tops with your choice of seeds. Transfer the tray to the top shelf of the oven, close the door. Bake for 12 minutes or until the rolls sound hollow when you tap them underneath.

Cheese and Bacon Bread

MAKES 1 LOAF

PREPARATION TIME 12 HOURS 30 MINUTES

COOKING TIME 35 MINUTES

INGREDIENTS

400 g / 14 oz / 2 ⅔ cups strong white bread flour, plus extra for dusting
½ tsp easy-blend dried yeast
1 tbsp caster (superfine) sugar
1 tsp fine sea salt
100 g / 3 ½ oz / 1 cup streaky bacon, chopped
100 g / 3 ½ oz / 1 cup Cheddar, grated
a small bunch of chives, chopped

METHOD

- Mix together the flour, yeast, sugar and salt. Stir the bacon, cheese and chives into 280 ml / 9 fl. oz / 1 cup of warm water and stir into the dry ingredients.
- Knead the mixture on a lightly oiled surface for 10 minutes or until the dough is smooth and elastic. Leave the dough to rest in a lightly oiled bowl, covered with oiled cling film, for 1–2 hours or until doubled in size.
- Knead the dough for 2 more minutes then roll it into a fat sausage. Turn it 90° and roll it tightly the other way then tuck the ends under and transfer the dough to a lined baking tray, keeping the seam underneath.
- Cover the dough loosely with oiled cling film and leave to prove for 45 minutes.
- Preheat the oven to 220°C (200°C fan) / 430F / gas 7.
- Transfer the tray to the top shelf of the oven. Bake for 35 minutes or until the underneath sounds hollow when tapped. Leave to cool completely on a wire rack before slicing.

Rye Bread

MAKES 1 LOAF

PREPARATION TIME 2 HOURS 30 MINUTES

COOKING TIME 35–40 MINUTES

INGREDIENTS

400 g / 14 oz / 2 ⅔ cups rye flour, plus extra for dusting
1 tsp easy-blend dried yeast
1 tbsp treacle
1 tbsp malt extract
1 tsp fine sea salt
1 tbsp olive oil

METHOD

- Mix together the flour, yeast, treacle, malt extract and salt. Stir the oil into 280 ml / 9 fl. oz / 1 cup of warm water. Stir the liquid into the dry ingredients then knead on a lightly oiled surface for 10 minutes or until the dough is smooth and elastic.
- Leave the dough to rest, covered with oiled cling film, for 1–2 hours or until doubled in size. Knead the dough for 2 more minutes, then shape it into a round loaf.
- Transfer the loaf to a greased baking tray and cover again with oiled cling film. Leave to prove for 1 hour or until doubled in size.
- Meanwhile, preheat the oven to 220°C (200°C fan) / 430F / gas 7. When the dough has risen, dust the top with flour.
- Transfer the tray to the top shelf of the oven, close the door. Bake for 35–40 minutes or until the loaf sounds hollow when tapped. Transfer the bread to a wire rack and leave to cool.

Seed-topped Wholemeal Rolls

MAKES 9 ROLLS
PREPARATION TIME 2 HOURS 30 MINUTES
COOKING TIME 12 MINUTES

INGREDIENTS

200 g / 7 oz / 1 ⅓ cups strong white bread flour, plus extra for dusting
200 g / 7 oz / 1 ⅓ cups stoneground wholemeal flour
½ tsp easy-blend dried yeast
1 tbsp caster (superfine) sugar
1 tsp fine sea salt
2 tbsp olive oil
2 tbsp milk
sesame seeds, poppy seeds and linseeds for sprinkling

METHOD

- Mix together the flours, yeast, sugar and salt. Stir the oil into 280 ml / 9 fl. oz / 1 cup of warm water then stir the liquid into the dry ingredients.
- Knead the mixture on a lightly oiled surface for 10 minutes or until smooth and elastic. Leave the dough to rest, covered with oiled cling film, for 1–2 hours or until doubled in size.
- Roll out the dough into a square, then cut it into 9 rolls and transfer to a greased baking tray. Cover the rolls with oiled cling film and leave to prove for 1 hour or until doubled in size.
- Preheat the oven to 220°C (200°C fan) / 430F / gas 7.
- Brush the rolls with milk and sprinkle the tops with your choice of seeds. Transfer the tray to the top shelf of the oven, close the door. Bake for 12 minutes or until the rolls sound hollow when you tap them underneath.

Baguettes

MAKES 12
PREPARATION TIME 2 HOURS 30 MINUTES
COOKING TIME 25 MINUTES

INGREDIENTS

350 g / 12 ½ oz / 1 ½ cups strong white bread flour, plus extra for dusting
50 g / 1 ¾ oz / ⅓ cup stoneground wholemeal flour
½ tsp easy-blend dried yeast
1 tbsp caster (superfine) sugar
1 tsp fine sea salt
1 tbsp olive oil

METHOD

- Mix together the flours, yeast, sugar and salt. Stir the oil into 280 ml / 9 fl. oz / 1 cup of warm water then stir it into the dry ingredients.
- Knead the mixture on a lightly oiled surface for 10 minutes or until smooth and elastic. Leave the dough to rest, covered with oiled cling film, for 1–2 hours or until doubled in size.
- Roll the dough into a long baguette, then make a diagonal cut half way down to form 2 shorter baguettes. Transfer the baguettes to a greased baking tray then cover with oiled cling film and leave to prove for 1 hour or until doubled in size.
- Preheat the oven to 220°C (200°C fan) / 425F / gas 7.
- Dust the baguettes with a little flour and make a few diagonal slashes along the top with a sharp knife. Transfer the tray to the top shelf of the oven.
- Bake for 25 minutes or until the baguettes sound hollow when you tap them underneath. Transfer to a wire rack and leave to cool completely before serving.

Wholemeal Granary Batons

MAKES 6

PREPARATION TIME 2 HOURS 30 MINUTES

COOKING TIME 20 MINUTES

INGREDIENTS

200 g / 7 oz / 1 ⅓ cups malted granary flour
200 g / 7 oz / 1 ⅓ cups wholemeal flour
1 tsp easy-blend dried yeast
2 tbsp caster (superfine) sugar
1 tsp fine sea salt
1 tbsp olive oil

METHOD

- Mix together the flours, yeast, sugar and salt. Stir the oil into 280 ml / 9 fl. oz / 1 cup of warm water then stir it into the dry ingredients.
- Knead the mixture on a lightly oiled surface with your hands for 10 minutes or until smooth and elastic. Leave the dough to rest in a lightly oiled bowl, covered with oiled cling film, for 1–2 hours or until doubled in size.
- Knead it for 2 more minutes then divide it into 6 pieces and shape into batons. Transfer the batons to a greased baking tray and cover with oiled cling film. Leave to prove for 1 hour or until doubled in size.
- Meanwhile, preheat the oven to 220°C (200°C fan) / 425F / gas 7.
- Slash the tops of the batons with a sharp knife. Transfer the tray to the top shelf of the oven, then close the door. Bake for 20 minutes or until the batons sound hollow when you tap them underneath. Transfer to a wire rack and leave to cool completely.

Crusty Walnut Rolls

MAKES 12

PREPARATION TIME 2 HOURS 30 MINUTES

COOKING TIME 12 MINUTES

INGREDIENTS

200 g / 7 oz / 1 ⅓ cups strong white bread flour, plus extra for dusting
200 g / 7 oz / 1 ⅓ cups stoneground wholemeal flour
½ tsp easy-blend dried yeast
1 tbsp caster (superfine) sugar
75 g / 2 ½ oz / ⅔ cup walnuts, chopped
1 tsp fine sea salt
2 tbsp olive oil

METHOD

- Mix together the flours, yeast, sugar, walnuts and salt. Stir the oil into 280 ml / 9 fl. oz / 1 cup of warm water then stir the liquid into the dry ingredients.
- Knead the mixture on a lightly oiled surface for 10 minutes or until smooth and elastic. Leave the dough to rest, covered with oiled cling film, for 1–2 hours or until doubled in size.
- Roll out the dough into a square, then cut it into 12 rectangular rolls and transfer to a greased baking tray. Cover the rolls with oiled cling film and leave to prove for 1 hour or until doubled in size.
- Preheat the oven to 220°C (200°C fan) / 430F / gas 7.
- Transfer the tray to the top shelf of the oven, close the door. Bake for 12 minutes or until the rolls sound hollow when you tap them underneath.

Long-ferment Bread

MAKES 1

PREPARATION TIME 14 HOURS 30 MINUTES

COOKING TIME 45 MINUTES

INGREDIENTS

200 g / 7 oz / 1 ⅓ cups strong white bread flour
200 g / 7 oz / 1 ⅓ cups wholemeal flour
4 tbsp rye flour
1 tsp easy-blend dried yeast
2 tbsp caster (superfine) sugar
1 tsp fine sea salt
1 tbsp olive oil

METHOD

- Mix together the flours, yeast, sugar and salt. Stir the oil into 280 ml / 9 fl. oz / 1 cup of warm water then stir it into the dry ingredients.
- Knead the mixture on a lightly oiled surface with your hands for 10 minutes or until smooth and elastic. Put the dough in a lightly oiled bowl, covered with oiled cling film, then put in the fridge for 6 hours or until doubled in size.
- Knead it for 2 more minutes then shape it into a round loaf. Transfer the loaf to a greased baking tray and cover with oiled cling film. Return to the fridge and leave to prove for 6 hours. Remove from the fridge and leave to come up to temperature and finish rising for 1–2 hours or until doubled in size.
- Meanwhile, preheat the oven to 220°C (200°C fan) / 425F / gas 7.
- Slash the top with a sharp knife. Transfer the tray to the top shelf of the oven, then close the door. Bake for 45 minutes or until the loaf sounds hollow when you tap it underneath. Transfer to a wire rack and leave to cool completely.

Seeded White Rolls

MAKES 8 ROLLS

PREPARATION TIME 2 HOURS 30 MINUTES

COOKING TIME 12 MINUTES

INGREDIENTS

400 g / 14 oz / 2 ⅔ cups strong white bread flour, plus extra for dusting
2 tbsp sunflower seeds
2 tbsp linseeds seeds
1 tbsp pumpkin seeds
½ tsp easy-blend dried yeast
1 tbsp caster (superfine) sugar
1 tsp fine sea salt
1 tbsp olive oil

METHOD

- Mix together the flour, seeds, yeast, sugar and salt. Stir the oil into 280 ml / 9 fl. oz / 1 cup of warm water then stir the liquid into the dry ingredients.
- Knead the mixture on a lightly oiled surface for 10 minutes or until smooth and elastic. Leave the dough to rest, covered with oiled cling film, for 1–2 hours or until doubled in size.
- Divide the dough into 8 evenly-sized pieces and shape into rolls on a greased baking tray. Cover the rolls with oiled cling film and leave to prove for 1 hour or until doubled in size.
- Preheat the oven to 220°C (200°C fan) / 430F / gas 7.
- Transfer the tray to the top shelf of the oven, close the door. Bake for 12 minutes or until the rolls sound hollow when you tap them underneath. Transfer the rolls to a wire rack and leave to cool completely.

Rustic Focaccia

MAKES 1

PREPARATION TIME 2 HOURS 30 MINUTES

COOKING TIME 25 MINUTES

INGREDIENTS

300 g / 10 ½ oz / 2 cups strong white bread flour

½ tsp easy-blend dried yeast

1 tsp fine sea salt

2 tbsp olive oil

METHOD

- Mix together the flour, yeast and salt. Stir the oil into 280 ml / 9 fl. oz / 1 cup of warm water then stir it into the dry ingredients.
- Knead the mixture on a lightly oiled surface for 10 minutes or until smooth and elastic. Leave the dough to rest, covered with oiled cling film, for 1–2 hours or until doubled in size.
- Oil a rectangular cake tin then stretch out the dough to cover the base. Cover the focaccia with oiled cling film and leave to prove for 1 hour or until doubled in size.
- Preheat the oven to 220°C (200°C fan) / 430F / gas 7.
- Transfer the tin to the top shelf of the oven, then close the door. Bake for 25 minutes or until the top is golden and the base is cooked through. Leave to cool completely on a wire rack.

Cheese Fougasse

MAKES 2

PREPARATION TIME 2 HOURS 30 MINUTES

COOKING TIME 25 MINUTES

INGREDIENTS

400 g / 14 oz / 2 ⅔ cups strong white bread flour, plus extra for dusting

½ tsp easy-blend dried yeast

4 tbsp parmesan, finely grated

1 tsp fine sea salt

3 tbsp olive oil, plus extra for brushing

150 g / 5 ½ oz / 1 ½ cups Gruyère, grated

METHOD

- Mix together the flours, yeast, parmesan and salt. Stir the oil into 280 ml / 9 fl. oz / 1 cup of warm water then stir it into the dry ingredients.
- Knead the mixture on a lightly oiled surface for 10 minutes or until smooth and elastic. Leave the dough to rest, covered with oiled cling film, for 1–2 hours or until doubled in size.
- Knead two-thirds of the Gruyère into the dough, then divide it into 2 pieces. Shape each piece into a leaf, making deep slashes where the veins would be. Transfer the fougasse to a greased baking tray then cover with oiled cling film and leave to prove for 1 hour or until doubled in size.
- Preheat the oven to 220°C (200°C fan) / 425F / gas 7.
- Sprinkle the rest of the cheese over the fougasse. Transfer the tray to the top shelf of the oven.
- Bake for 25 minutes or until the bread sounds hollow when you tap it underneath. Transfer to a wire rack and brush with olive oil, then leave to cool completely before serving.

Hazelnut and Fig Rolls

MAKES 12

PREPARATION TIME 2 HOURS 30 MINUTES

COOKING TIME 15 MINUTES

INGREDIENTS

400 g / 14 oz / 2 ⅔ cups strong white bread flour, plus extra for dusting
½ tsp easy-blend dried yeast
1 tbsp caster (superfine) sugar
1 tsp fine sea salt
75 g / 2 ½ oz / ⅓ cup dried figs, chopped
50 g 1 ¾ oz / ½ cup hazelnuts (cobnuts), chopped
1 tbsp olive oil

METHOD

- Mix together the flour, yeast, sugar, salt, figs and hazelnuts. Stir the oil into 280 ml / 9 fl. oz / 1 cup of warm water then stir it into the dry ingredients.
- Knead the mixture on a lightly oiled surface for 10 minutes or until smooth and elastic. Leave the dough to rest, covered with oiled cling film, for 1–2 hours or until doubled in size.
- Shape the dough into 12 rolls and transfer to a greased baking tray, then cover with oiled cling film and leave to prove for 1 hour or until doubled in size.
- Preheat the oven to 220°C (200°C fan) / 425F / gas 7.
- Dust the rolls with a little flour and slash the top of each one with a sharp knife. Transfer the tray to the top shelf of the oven, then close the door.
- Bake for 15 minutes or until the rolls sound hollow when you tap them underneath. Transfer to a wire rack and leave to cool completely before serving.

Cakes and Muffins

Mixed Fruit Scones

MAKES 12

PREPARATION TIME 25 MINUTES

COOKING TIME 15–20 MINUTES

INGREDIENTS

225 g / 8 oz / 1 ½ cups self-raising flour
55 g / 2 oz / ¼ cup butter
75 g / 2 ½ oz / ½ cup mixed dried fruit
150 ml / 5 fl. oz / ⅔ cup whole milk

METHOD

- Preheat the oven to 220°C (200°C fan) / 425F / gas 7 and oil a large baking sheet.
- Sieve the flour into a bowl and rub in the butter until the mixture resembles fine breadcrumbs. Add the mixed fruit and stir in enough milk to bring the mixture together into a soft dough.
- Flatten the dough with your hands on a floured work surface into a 2.5 cm (1 in) thick rectangle. Transfer it to the baking sheet and score into 12 squares.
- Bake in the oven for 15–20 minutes or until golden brown and cooked through. Transfer the scones to a wire rack to cool a little, then break into squares and serve with jam.

Chocolate and Hazelnut Palmiers

MAKES 12

PREPARATION TIME 15 MINUTES

COOKING TIME 20 MINUTES

INGREDIENTS

250 g / 9 oz / 1 cup all-butter puff pastry
100 g / 3 ½ oz / ½ cup chocolate and hazelnut (cobnut) spread

METHOD

- Preheat the oven to 220°C (200°C fan) / 430F / gas 7 and line a baking tray with non-stick baking paper.
- Roll out the pastry on a floured surface into a large rectangle. Spread the top of the pastry with chocolate and hazelnut spread, then roll it up into a tight sausage. Cut the roll across into 12 slices, then transfer them to the prepared baking tray.
- Bake in the oven for 20 minutes or until golden brown and cooked through. Transfer the pastries to a wire rack to cool a little and serve warm.

Oat and Cranberry Muffins

MAKES 12

PREPARATION TIME 25 MINUTES

COOKING TIME 20–25 MINUTES

INGREDIENTS

1 large egg
120 ml / 4 fl. oz / ½ cup sunflower oil
120 ml / 4 fl. oz / ½ cup milk
375 g / 12 ½ oz / 2 ½ cups wholemeal self-raising flour, sifted
1 tsp baking powder
1 tsp mixed spice
200 g / 7 oz / ¾ cup caster (superfine) sugar
75 g / 2 ½ oz / ½ cup dried cranberries
75 g / 2 ½ oz / ½ cup porridge oats

METHOD

- Preheat the oven to 180°C (160°C fan) / 350F / gas 4 and line 12 mini pudding basins with squares of greaseproof paper.
- Beat the egg in a jug with the oil and milk until well mixed. Mix the flour, baking powder, spice, sugar, cranberries and oats in a bowl, then pour in the egg mixture and stir just enough to combine.
- Divide the mixture between the paper cases, then bake in the oven for 20–25 minutes. Test with a wooden toothpick, if it comes out clean, the cakes are done. Leave to cool before serving.

Cherry and Hazelnut Muffins

MAKES 12

PREPARATION TIME 20 MINUTES

COOKING TIME 20–25 MINUTES

INGREDIENTS

1 large egg
1 orange, zest finely grated
125 ml / 4 ½ fl. oz / ½ cup sunflower oil
125 ml / 4 ½ fl. oz / ½ cup milk
375 g / 13 oz / 2 ½ cups self-raising flour, sifted
1 tsp baking powder
200 g / 7 oz / ¾ cup caster (superfine) sugar
75 g / 2 ½ oz / ⅓ cup glacé cherries, quartered
50 g / 1 ¾ oz / ½ cup hazelnuts (cobnuts), chopped

METHOD

- Preheat the oven to 180°C (160°C fan) / 350F / gas 4 and grease a 12-square-hole silicone muffin mould.
- Beat the egg in a jug with the orange zest, oil and milk until well mixed.
- Mix the flour, baking powder and sugar in a bowl, then pour in the egg mixture, chopped cherries and hazelnuts and stir just enough to combine.
- Spoon the mixture into the mould, then bake in the oven for 20–25 minutes. Test with a wooden toothpick, if it comes out clean, the cakes are done. Transfer the cakes to a wire rack and leave to cool completely.

Apple Mini Muffins

MAKES 12

PREPARATION TIME 25 MINUTES

COOKING TIME 15–20 MINUTES

INGREDIENTS

1 large egg
120 ml / 4 fl. oz / ½ cup sunflower oil
120 ml / 4 fl. oz / ½ cup milk
375 g / 12 ½ oz / 2 ½ cups self-raising flour, sifted
1 tsp baking powder
1 tsp ground ginger
200 g / 7 oz / ¾ cup caster (superfine) sugar
150 g / 5 oz / 1 cup eating apple, thinly sliced

METHOD

- Preheat the oven to 180°C (160°C fan) / 350F / gas 4 and line a 12-hole cupcake tin with paper cases.
- Beat the egg in a jug with the oil and milk until well mixed. Mix the flour, baking powder, ginger and sugar in a bowl, then pour in the egg mixture and stir just enough to combine. Reserve 12 apple slices and fold the rest into the mixture.
- Divide the mixture between the paper cases and top with the reserved apple slices, then bake in the oven for 15–20 minutes.
- Test with a wooden toothpick, if it comes out clean, the cakes are done. Transfer the cakes to a wire rack and leave to cool completely.

Wholemeal Blueberry Muffins

MAKES 12

PREPARATION TIME 25 MINUTES

COOKING TIME 20–25 MINUTES

INGREDIENTS

1 large egg
120 ml / 4 fl. oz / ½ cup sunflower oil
120 ml / 4 fl. oz / ½ cup whole milk
375 g / 12 ½ oz / 2 ½ cups wholemeal self-raising flour, sifted
1 tsp baking powder
1 tsp mixed spice
200 g / 7 oz / ¾ cup caster (superfine) sugar
100 g / 3 ½ oz / ⅔ cup blueberries
2 tbsp sugar nibs

METHOD

- Preheat the oven to 180°C (160°C fan) / 350F / gas 4 and line 12 mini pudding basins with squares of greaseproof paper.
- Beat the egg in a jug with the oil and milk until well mixed. Mix the flour, baking powder, spice, sugar and blueberries in a bowl, then pour in the egg mixture and stir just enough to combine.
- Divide the mixture between the paper cases and sprinkle with sugar nibs, then bake in the oven for 20–25 minutes. Test with a wooden toothpick, if it comes out clean, the cakes are done. Leave to cool before serving.

Raisin Scones with Cream and Jam

MAKES 12

PREPARATION TIME 25 MINUTES

COOKING TIME 15 MINUTES

INGREDIENTS

225 g / 8 oz / 1 ½ cups self-raising flour

55 g / 2 oz / ¼ cup butter, plus extra for spreading

75 g / 2 ½ oz / ⅓ cup raisins

150 ml / 5 fl. oz / ⅔ cup whole milk

1 egg, beaten

200 g / 7 oz / ¾ cup double (heavy) cream

200 g / 7 oz / ¾ cup strawberry jam (jelly)

METHOD

- Preheat the oven to 220°C (200°C fan) / 425F / gas 7 and oil a large baking sheet.
- Sieve the flour into a bowl and rub in the butter until the mixture resembles fine breadcrumbs. Stir in the raisins with enough milk to bring the mixture together into a soft dough.
- Flatten the dough with your hands on a floured work surface until 2.5 cm (1 in) thick. Use a pastry cutter to cut out 12 circles and transfer them to the prepared baking sheet.
- Brush the scones with beaten egg then bake for 15 minutes or until golden brown and cooked through. Transfer the scones to a wire rack to cool completely.
- Whip the cream until it just holds its shape. When the scones have cooled, spread them with butter and jam, then spoon a little whipped cream on top.

Chocolate Chip Cupcakes with Blueberries

MAKES 6

PREPARATION TIME 35 MINUTES

COOKING TIME 15–20 MINUTES

INGREDIENTS

110 g / 4 oz / ⅔ cup self-raising flour, sifted
1 tsp baking powder
110 g / 4 oz / ½ cup caster (superfine) sugar
110 g / 4 oz / ½ cup butter, softened
2 large eggs
1 tsp vanilla extract
75 g / 2 ½ oz / ½ cup chocolate chips

TO DECORATE

100 g / 3 ½ oz / 1 cup icing (confectioners') sugar
100 g / 3 ½ oz / ⅔ cup blueberries

METHOD

- Preheat the oven to 190°C (170°C fan) / 375F / gas 5 and line a 6-hole muffin tin with paper cases.
- Combine the flour, baking powder, sugar, butter, eggs and vanilla extract in a bowl and whisk together for 2 minutes or until smooth. Stir in the chocolate chips.
- Divide the mixture between the cases, then transfer the tin to the oven and bake for 20–25 minutes. Test with a wooden toothpick, if it comes out clean, the cakes are done. Transfer the cakes to a wire rack and leave to cool completely.
- Add cold water a few drops at a time to the icing sugar until you get a pourable icing, then spoon it over the cakes and sprinkle with blueberries.

Madeleines

MAKES 12

PREPARATION TIME 1 HOUR 15 MINUTES

COOKING TIME 10–15 MINUTES

INGREDIENTS

110 g / 4 oz / ½ cup butter
55 g / 2 oz / ⅓ cup plain (all purpose) flour
55 g / 2 oz / ½ cup ground almonds
110 g / 4 oz / 1 cup icing (confectioners') sugar
3 large egg whites

METHOD

- Heat the butter until it foams and starts to smell nutty, then leave to cool.
- Combine the flour, ground almonds and icing sugar in a bowl and whisk in the egg whites. Pour the cooled butter through a sieve into the bowl and whisk into the mixture until evenly mixed. Leave the cake mixture to rest in the fridge for an hour.
- Preheat the oven to 170°C (150°C fan) / 325F / gas 3 and oil and flour a 12-hole madeleine mould.
- Spoon the mixture into the moulds, then transfer the tin to the oven and bake for 10–15 minutes. Test with a wooden toothpick, if it comes out clean, the cakes are done. Transfer the cakes to a wire rack to cool.

Almond Choux Buns

MAKES 8

PREPARATION TIME 45 MINUTES

COOKING TIME 20 MINUTES

INGREDIENTS

55 g / 2 oz / ¼ cup butter, cubed
70 g / 2 ½ oz / ½cup strong white bread flour, sieved
2 large eggs, beaten
50 g / 2 ½ oz / ⅔ cup flaked (slivered) almonds
225 ml / 8 fl. oz double (heavy) cream
4 tbsp Amaretto liqueur
icing (confectioners') sugar to dust

METHOD

- Preheat the oven to 200°C (180°C fan) / 400F / gas 6.
- Oil and line a large baking tray with greaseproof paper, then spray it with water.
- Bring the butter and 150 ml / 5 fl. oz / ⅔ cup cold water to the boil then beat in the flour off the heat. Continue to beat until you have a smooth ball of pastry that leaves the sides of the saucepan clean. Stir in the beaten egg a little at a time to make a glossy paste.
- Spoon the pastry into a piping bag fitted with a large star nozzle and pipe 8 buns onto the tray. Sprinkle with almonds and bake for 20 minutes, increasing the heat to 220°C (200°C fan) / 425F / gas 7 halfway through.
- Transfer the choux buns to a wire rack, cut in half horizontally and leave to cool completely.
- Whip the cream with the Amaretto until thick then spoon into a piping bag fitted with a large star nozzle. Sandwich the choux buns back together with the cream, then dust liberally with icing sugar.

Almond Pain au Chocolat

MAKES 6

PREPARATION TIME 15 MINUTES

COOKING TIME 10 MINUTES

INGREDIENTS

55 g / 2 oz / ½ cup ground almonds
55 g / 2 oz / ¼ cup caster (superfine) sugar
55 g / 2 oz / ¼ cup butter, softened
1 large egg
½ tsp almond essence
6 pain au chocolat
3 tbsp flaked (slivered) almonds
icing (confectioners') sugar for dusting

METHOD

- Preheat the oven to 200°C (180°C fan) / 400F / gas 6.
- Combine the ground almonds, sugar, butter, egg and almond essence in a bowl and whisk together for 2 minutes or until smooth.
- Cut open each pain au chocolat and spread a spoonful of the almond mixture inside. Transfer to a baking tray and spoon the rest of the mixture over the top.
- Sprinkle with flaked almonds and bake for 10 minutes or until the tops are golden brown. Dust with icing sugar before serving.

Chocolate and Hazelnut Mini Cupcakes

MAKES 24

PREPARATION TIME 15 MINUTES

COOKING TIME 12–15 MINUTES

INGREDIENTS

110 g / 4 oz / ⅔ cup self-raising flour, sifted
110 g / 4 oz / ½ cup caster (superfine) sugar
110 g / 4 oz / ½ cup butter, softened
2 large eggs
2 tbsp unsweetened cocoa powder
50 g / 1 ¾ oz / ½ cup hazelnuts (cobnuts), chopped

METHOD

- Preheat the oven to 190°C (170°C fan) / 375F / gas 5 and line a 24-hole mini cupcake tin with paper cases.
- Combine the flour, sugar, butter, eggs, cocoa powder and three quarters of the hazelnuts in a bowl and whisk together for 2 minutes or until smooth.
- Divide the mixture between the cases, then transfer the tin to the oven and bake for 12–15 minutes. Test with a wooden toothpick, if it comes out clean, the cakes are done.
- Transfer the cakes to a wire rack, sprinkle over the rest of the hazelnuts and leave to cool completely.

Chocolate Chip and Oat Bran Muffins

MAKES 12

PREPARATION TIME 15 MINUTES

COOKING TIME 20–25 MINUTES

INGREDIENTS

1 large egg
120 ml / 4 fl. oz / ½ cup sunflower oil
120 ml / 4 fl. oz / ½ cup milk
375 g / 12 ½ oz / 2 ½ cups wholemeal self-raising flour, sifted
1 tsp baking powder
200 g / 7 oz / ¾ cup caster (superfine) sugar
75 g / 2 ½ oz / ½ cup chocolate chips
4 tbsp oat bran

METHOD

- Preheat the oven to 180°C (160°C fan) / 350F / gas 4 and line a 12-hole muffin tin with muffin wrappers.
- Beat the egg in a jug with the oil and milk until well mixed. Mix the flour, baking powder, sugar, chocolate chips and half of the oat bran in a bowl, then pour in the egg mixture and stir just enough to combine.
- Divide the mixture between the wrappers and sprinkle the tops with the rest of the oat bran, then bake in the oven for 20–25 minutes. Test with a wooden toothpick, if it comes out clean, the cakes are done. Leave to cool before serving.

Chocolate and Sesame Muffins

MAKES 12

PREPARATION TIME 15 MINUTES

COOKING TIME 20–25 MINUTES

INGREDIENTS

1 large egg
100 ml / 3 ½ fl. oz / ½ cup sunflower oil
2 tbsp sesame oil
125 ml / 4 ½ fl. oz / ½ cup milk
350 g / 12 ½ oz / 2 ⅓ cups self-raising flour, sifted
50 g / 1 ¾ oz / ½ cup unsweetened cocoa powder, sifted
1 tsp baking powder
200 g / 7 oz / ¾ cup caster (superfine) sugar
3 tbsp sesame seeds

METHOD

- Preheat the oven to 180°C (160°C fan) / 350F / gas 4 and grease 12 mini pudding basins.
- Beat the egg in a jug with the oils and milk until well mixed.
- Mix the flour, cocoa, baking powder and sugar in a bowl, then pour in the egg mixture and stir just enough to combine.
- Divide the mixture between the cases and sprinkle with sesame seeds, then bake in the oven for 20–25 minutes. Test with a wooden toothpick, if it comes out clean, the cakes are done. Serve warm or leave to cool on a wire rack.

Ginger Cupcakes with Ginger Buttercream

MAKES 12

PREPARATION TIME 45 MINUTES

COOKING TIME 15–20 MINUTES

INGREDIENTS

110 g / 4 oz / ⅔ cup self-raising flour, sifted
110 g / 4 oz / ½ cup caster (superfine) sugar
110 g / 4 oz / ½ cup butter, softened
2 tsp ground ginger
2 large eggs
3 pieces of stem ginger, finely chopped
2 tbsp syrup from the stem ginger jar

TO DECORATE

100 g / 3 ½ oz / ½ cup butter, softened
200 g / 7 oz / 2 cups icing (confectioners') sugar
1 tbsp stem ginger syrup
1 tsp ground ginger
2 ginger-nut biscuits, crumbled

METHOD

- Preheat the oven to 190°C (170°C fan) / 375F / gas 5 and line a 12-hole cupcake tin with paper cases.
- Combine the flour, sugar, butter, ground ginger, eggs and stem ginger in a bowl and whisk together for 2 minutes or until smooth.
- Divide the mixture between the cases, then transfer the tin to the oven and bake for 15–20 minutes. Test with a wooden toothpick, if it comes out clean, the cakes are done.
- Transfer the cakes to a wire rack, brush with ginger syrup and leave to cool completely.
- Beat the butter until smooth, then gradually whisk in the icing sugar, ginger syrup and ground ginger. Spoon the buttercream into a piping bag, fitted with a large plain nozzle, and pipe it onto the cakes. Crumble over the ginger-nut biscuits.

Plain Buttercream Cupcakes

MAKES 12

PREPARATION TIME 45 MINUTES

COOKING TIME 15–20 MINUTES

INGREDIENTS

110 g / 4 oz / ⅔ cup self-raising flour, sifted
110 g / 4 oz / ½ cup caster (superfine) sugar
110 g / 4 oz / ½ cup butter, softened
2 large eggs
1 tsp vanilla extract

TO DECORATE

100 g / 3 ½ oz / ½ cup butter, softened
200 g / 7 oz / 2 cups icing (confectioners') sugar

METHOD

- Preheat the oven to 190°C (170°C fan) / 375F / gas 5 and line a 12-hole cupcake tin with paper cases.
- Combine the flour, sugar, butter, eggs and vanilla extract in a bowl and whisk together for 2 minutes or until smooth.
- Divide the mixture between the cases, then transfer the tin to the oven and bake for 15–20 minutes. Test with a wooden toothpick, if it comes out clean, the cakes are done. Transfer the cakes to a wire rack and leave to cool completely.
- Beat the butter until smooth, then gradually whisk in the icing sugar. If the icing is too stiff, add a teaspoon or two of warm water and beat well. Use a palette knife to spread the buttercream onto the cakes.

Strawberry Eclairs

MAKES 12

PREPARATION TIME 45 MINUTES

COOKING TIME 20 MINUTES

INGREDIENTS

55 g / 2 oz / ¼ cup butter, cubed

70 g / 2 ½ oz / ½ cup strong white bread flour, sieved

2 large eggs, beaten

FOR THE FILLING

600 ml / 1 pint / 2 ½ cups double (heavy) cream

2 tbsp icing (confectioners') sugar, plus extra for dusting

200 g / 7 oz / 1 ⅓ cups strawberries, hulled

METHOD

- Preheat the oven to 200°C (180°C fan) / 400F / gas 6. Oil and line a large baking tray with greaseproof paper, then spray it with a little water.
- Put the butter in a saucepan with 150 ml / 5 fl. oz / ⅔ cup cold water and heat until the butter melts and the water starts to boil. Turn off the heat and beat in the flour. Continue to beat the mixture until it forms a smooth ball of pastry. Stir in the beaten egg a little at a time until you have a glossy paste.
- Spoon the pastry into a piping bag with a large plain nozzle and pipe 12 cm (5 in) lines onto the prepared baking tray.
- Bake for 10 minutes, then increase the heat to 220°C (200°C fan) / 425F / gas 7 and bake for another 10 minutes. Transfer to a wire rack and slice down one side of each one so the steam can escape. Leave to cool completely.
- Whip the cream with the icing sugar until thick. Spoon the cream into a piping bag fitted with a large star nozzle and fill the eclairs then stud each one with strawberries. Dust the tops with icing sugar just before serving.

Profiteroles

MAKES 24

PREPARATION TIME 45 MINUTES

COOKING TIME 20 MINUTES

INGREDIENTS

55 g / 2 oz / ¼ cup butter, cubed
75 g / 2 ½ oz / ½ cup strong white bread flour, sieved
2 large eggs, beaten
225 ml / 8 fl. oz / 1 cup double (heavy) cream
100 g / 3 ½ oz / 1 cup icing (confectioners') sugar
100 ml / 3 ½ fl. oz / ½ cup chocolate sauce
2 tbsp white chocolate sprinkles

METHOD

- Preheat the oven to 200°C (180°C fan) / 400F / gas 6. Line a baking tray with greaseproof paper and spray with a little water.
- Melt the butter with 150 ml / 5 fl. oz / ⅔ cup water and bring to the boil. Turn off the heat. Immediately beat in the flour with a wooden spoon until it forms a smooth ball of pastry. Incorporate the egg a little at a time to make a glossy paste.
- Spoon the pastry into a piping bag fitted with a large plain nozzle and pipe 2.5 cm (1 in) buns onto the baking tray.
- Bake for 20 minutes, increasing the temperature to 220°C (200°C fan) / 425F / gas 7 halfway through. Transfer to a wire rack and make a hole in the underneath of each one so the steam can escape. Leave to cool completely.
- Whip the cream until thick, then spoon it into a piping bag and fill the choux buns through the steam hole.
- Stir a few drops of water into the icing sugar until you get a pourable icing then drizzle it over the profiteroles. Squeeze over the chocolate sauce then sprinkle with white chocolate sprinkles.

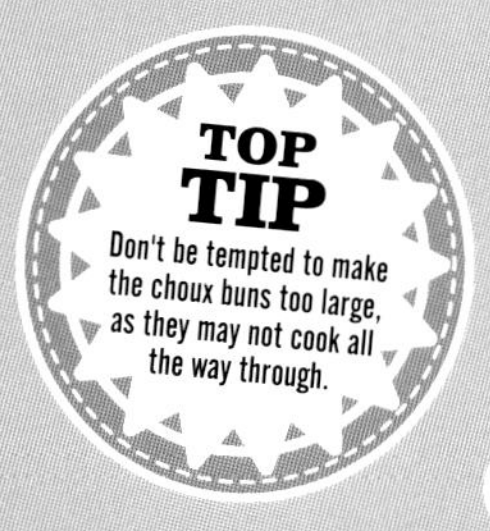

Lemon Meringue Pies

MAKES 6
PREPARATION TIME 1 HOUR
COOKING TIME 30 MINUTES

INGREDIENTS

100 g / 3 ½ oz / ½ cup butter, cubed
200 g / 7 oz / 1 ⅓ cups plain (all purpose) flour
225 g / 8 oz / 1 cup lemon curd
4 large egg whites
110g / 4 oz / ½ cup caster (superfine) sugar

METHOD

- Preheat the oven to 200°C (180°C fan) / 400F / gas 6.
- Rub the butter into the flour and add just enough cold water to bind. Chill for 30 minutes then roll out on a floured surface and cut out 6 circles with a large round cookie cutter. Use the pastry circles to line a 6-hole deep muffin tin and prick the bases with a fork.
- Line the pastry with cling film and fill with baking beans or rice then bake for 10 minutes. Remove the cling film and beans and cook for another 8 minutes to crisp. Fill the pastry cases with lemon curd.
- Whisk the egg whites until stiff, then gradually add the sugar and whisk until the mixture is thick and shiny. Spoon the meringue into a piping bag fitted with a large star nozzle and pipe a swirl on top of each pie. Return the tin to the oven to bake for 10 minutes or until golden brown. Serve hot or cold.

Lemon and Chocolate Tray Bake

MAKES 9 SQUARES

PREPARATION TIME 1 HOUR

COOKING TIME 30 MINUTES

INGREDIENTS

2 tsp cornflour (cornstarch)
4 lemons, zest and juice
4 large eggs, beaten
225 g / 8 oz / 1 cup butter
175 g / 6 oz / ¾ cup caster (superfine) sugar

FOR THE PASTRY

100 g / 3 ½ oz / ½ cup butter, cubed
200 g / 7 oz / 1 ⅓ cups plain (all purpose) flour
55 g / 2 oz / ½ cup caster (superfine) sugar
1 egg, beaten

TO DECORATE

200 g / 7 oz / 1 ¼ cups dark chocolate (minimum 70% cocoa solids), chopped
50 g / 1 ¾ oz / ½ cup butter

METHOD

- Preheat the oven to 200°C (180°C fan) / 390F / gas 6.
- Rub the butter into the flour and sugar then add the egg with just enough cold water to bind. Wrap the dough in cling film and chill for 30 minutes then roll out on a floured surface.
- Use the pastry to line the bottom of a 23 cm (9 in) square cake tin and trim the edges. Prick the pastry with a fork, line with cling film and fill with baking beans or rice. Bake for 10 minutes then remove the cling film and baking beans and cook for another 8 minutes.
- Meanwhile, dissolve the cornflour in the lemon juice and put it in a saucepan with the rest of the ingredients. Stir over a medium heat after 6 or 7 minutes the mixture should thicken. Continue until it starts to bubble then spoon it onto the pastry base and level with a palette knife. Leave to cool completely.
- Put the chocolate and butter in a bowl set over a pan of simmering water and stir together until melted.
- Pour the mixture over the lemon layer and leave to cool and set before cutting into 9 squares.

Chocolate and Hazelnut Brownies

MAKES 16

PREPARATION TIME 5 MINUTES

COOKING TIME 35 MINUTES

INGREDIENTS

110 g / 4 oz / ⅔ cup dark chocolate (minimum 70% cocoa solids), chopped

85 g / 3 oz / ¾ cup unsweetened cocoa powder, sifted

225 g / 8 oz / 1 cup butter

450 g / 1 lb / 2 ½ cups light brown sugar

4 large eggs

110 g / 4 oz / 1 cup self-raising flour

75 g / 2 ½ oz / ½ cup toasted hazelnuts (cobnuts), chopped

METHOD

- Preheat the oven to 160°C (140°C fan) / 325F / gas 3 and oil and line a 20 cm x 20 cm (8 in x 8 in) square cake tin.
- Melt the chocolate, cocoa and butter together in a saucepan, then leave to cool a little.
- Whisk the sugar and eggs together with an electric whisk for 3 minutes or until very light and creamy.
- Pour in the chocolate mixture and sieve over the flour. Reserve 1 tbsp of the nuts to decorate and fold the rest into the brownie batter.
- Scrape into the tin and bake for 35 minutes or until the outside is set, but the centre is still quite soft.
- Leave the brownie to cool completely before cutting into 12 squares and sprinkling with the reserved hazelnuts.

Blueberry and Orange Polenta Cake

MAKES 8

PREPARATION TIME 20 MINUTES

COOKING TIME 45 MINUTES

INGREDIENTS

200 g / 7 oz / ¾ cup butter
200 g / 7 oz / ¾ cup caster (superfine) sugar
3 large eggs
2 oranges, zest finely grated
125 g / 4 ½ oz / ¾ cup quick-cook polenta
250 g/ 9 oz / 2 ½ cups ground almonds
50 g / 1 ¾ oz / ⅓ cup cornflour (cornstarch)
2 tsp ground ginger
2 tsp baking powder
100 g / 3 ½ oz / ⅔ cup blueberries, plus extra to serve
icing (confectioners') sugar for dusting

METHOD

- Preheat the oven to 180°C (160°C fan) / 355F / gas 4 and grease a 23 cm (9 in) round cake tin.
- Cream the butter and sugar together until smooth and pale. Lightly beat the eggs with the orange zest, then gradually beat them into the butter and sugar mixture. Mix the polenta with the ground almonds, cornflour, ground ginger and baking powder, then add it slowly to the mix, stopping as soon as everything is smoothly combined.
- Fold in the blueberries, then scrape the mixture into the tin and level the top with a spatula. Bake for 45 minutes or until a skewer inserted into the centre comes out clean.
- Dust with icing sugar and serve warm or cold with extra blueberries.

Wholemeal Walnut Loaf Cake

SERVES 8

PREPARATION TIME 15 MINUTES

COOKING TIME 35–40 MINUTES

INGREDIENTS

100 g / 3 ½ oz / ⅔ cup stoneground wholemeal flour
50 g / 1 ¾ oz / ½ cup ground walnuts
2 tsp baking powder
150 g / 5 ½ oz / ⅔ cup caster (superfine) sugar
150 g / 5 ½ oz / ⅔ cup butter
3 large eggs
1 tsp ground cinnamon
1 tsp ground ginger
½ tsp freshly grated nutmeg
8 walnut halves
pouring cream to serve

METHOD

- Preheat the oven to 180°C (160°C fan) / 355F / gas 4 and grease and line a small loaf tin.
- Put all of the ingredients, except for the walnut halves, in a large mixing bowl and whisk them together with an electric whisk for 4 minutes or until pale and well whipped.
- Scrape the mixture into the tin and level the top with a spatula, then lay the walnut halves on top in a line down the middle.
- Bake for 35–40 minutes. The cake is ready when a toothpick inserted in the centre comes out clean. Transfer the cake to a wire rack to cool completely before slicing and serving with pouring cream.

Orange Syrup Loaf Cake

SERVES 8

PREPARATION TIME 30 MINUTES

COOKING TIME 55 MINUTES

INGREDIENTS

225 g / 8 oz / 1 ½ cups self-raising flour
100 g / 3 ½ oz / ½ cup butter, cubed
85 g / 3 oz / ⅓ cup caster (superfine) sugar
2 oranges, juiced and zest finely grated
1 large egg

FOR THE TOPPING

2 oranges, juiced
100 g / 3 ½ oz / ½ cup caster (superfine) sugar
8 candied orange slices

METHOD

- Preheat the oven to 180°C (160°C fan) / 355F / gas 4 and line a loaf tin with non-stick baking paper.
- Sieve the flour into a mixing bowl and rub in the butter until it resembles fine breadcrumbs, then stir in the sugar and orange zest. Lightly beat the egg with the orange juice and stir it into the dry ingredients until just combined.
- Scrape the mixture into the loaf tin and bake for 55 minutes or until a skewer inserted in the centre comes out clean.
- While the cake is cooking, put the sugar and orange juice into a small saucepan and stir over a low heat until the sugar dissolves. Increase the heat and simmer without stirring for 4 minutes or until syrupy. Stir in the candied orange slices.
- When the cake comes out of the oven, arrange the orange slices on top and spoon over the hot syrup. Leave to soak until the cake has cooled completely before unmoulding.

Lemon and Poppy Seed Cake

SERVES 8

PREPARATION TIME 15 MINUTES

COOKING TIME 55 MINUTES

INGREDIENTS

225 g / 8 oz / 1 ½ cups self-raising flour
100 g / 3 ½ oz / ½ cup butter, cubed
100 g / 3 ½ oz / ½ cup caster (superfine) sugar
3 tbsp poppy seeds
1 large egg
75 ml / 2 ½ fl. oz / ⅓ cup whole milk
1 lemon, juiced and zest finely grated

METHOD

- Preheat the oven to 180°C (160°C fan) / 355F / gas 4 and line a 18 cm (7 in) round cake tin with non-stick baking paper.
- Sieve the flour into a mixing bowl and rub in the butter until it resembles fine breadcrumbs then stir in the sugar and poppy seeds.
- Lightly beat the egg with the milk, lemon juice and lemon zest and stir it into the dry ingredients until just combined.
- Scrape the mixture into the tin and bake for 55 minutes or until a skewer inserted into the centre comes out clean. Transfer the cake to a wire rack and leave to cool completely.

Toffee and nut-topped Ginger Cake

SERVES 8

PREPARATION TIME 30 MINUTES

COOKING TIME 35–40 MINUTES

INGREDIENTS

250 g / 9 oz / 1 ⅔ cups self-raising flour
1 tsp bicarbonate of (baking) soda
2 tsp ground ginger
150 g / 5 ½ oz / ½ cup golden syrup
50 g / 1 ¾ oz / ¼ cup treacle
125 g / 4 ½ oz / ½ cup butter
125 g / 4 ½ oz / ¾ cup dark brown sugar
2 large eggs, beaten
250 ml / 9 fl. oz / 1 cup milk

FOR THE TOPPING

85 g / 3 oz / ½ cup butter
85 g / 3 oz / ¼ cup golden syrup
85 g / 3 oz / ½ cup dark brown sugar
50 g / 1 ¾ oz / ½ cup walnuts, chopped
50 g / 1 ¾ oz / ½ cup hazelnuts (cobnuts), chopped

METHOD

- Preheat the oven to 180°C (160°C fan) / 355F / gas 4 and grease and line a loaf tin.
- Sieve the flour, bicarbonate of soda and ginger into a bowl. Put the golden syrup, treacle, butter and brown sugar in a small saucepan and boil gently for 2 minutes, stirring to dissolve the sugar. Add the butter and sugar mixture to the flour with the eggs and milk and fold it all together until smooth.
- Scrape the mixture into the prepared tin and bake for 35–40 minutes. The cake is ready when a toothpick inserted in the centre comes out clean. Transfer the cake to a wire rack to cool completely.
- To make the topping, put the butter, syrup and sugar in a saucepan and stir over a low heat to dissolve the sugar. Increase the heat and simmer without stirring for 3 minutes or until thick. Stir in the nuts then leave to cool a little before spooning it over the cake.

Blueberry Bundt Cakes

MAKES 8

PREPARATION TIME 15 MINUTES

COOKING TIME 25 MINUTES

INGREDIENTS

225 g / 8 oz / 1 cup butter, softened
225 g / 8 oz / 1 cup caster (superfine) sugar
4 large eggs, beaten
150 g / 5 ½ oz / 1 cup self-raising flour
75 g / 2 ½ oz / ½ cup blueberries

METHOD

- Preheat the oven to 180°C (160°C fan) / 350F / gas 4 and butter 8 mini bundt tins or other decorative moulds.
- Cream the butter and sugar together until well whipped then whisk in the eggs in four batches, beating well after each addition.
- Fold in the flour and blueberries then divide the mixture between the tins. Bake the cakes for 25 minutes or until a skewer inserted in the centre comes out clean. Turn the cakes out onto a wire rack and leave to cool completely.

Giant Rum Baba

SERVES 6

PREPARATION TIME 2 HOURS

COOKING TIME 20–30 MINUTES

INGREDIENTS

150 g / 5 oz / 1 cup plain (all purpose) flour
2 tsp easy-blend dried yeast
1 tbsp caster (superfine) sugar
½ tsp salt
3 large eggs, lightly beaten
75 g / 2 ½ oz / ⅓ cup butter, softened

FOR THE SOAKING SYRUP

450 g / 1 lb / 2 cups caster (superfine) sugar
250 ml / 9 fl. oz / 1 cup rum

TO DECORATE

250 ml / 9 fl. oz / 1 cup double (heavy) cream
½ papaya, peeled, deseeded and thinly sliced
4 strawberries, sliced
6 raspberries, halved

METHOD

- Oil a 23 cm (9 in) ring mould. Combine the flour, yeast, sugar and salt in a bowl and gradually whisk in half of the beaten egg with an electric whisk. Continuing to whisk, incorporate half of the butter, followed by the rest of the egg. Beat the remaining butter in with a wooden spoon, then spoon the mixture into the mould.
- Leave the baba to prove in a warm, draught-free place for 1 hour or until it has double in size. Preheat the oven to 200°C (180°C fan) / 400F / gas 6.
- Bake the baba for 20–30 minutes or until golden brown and cooked through, then turn it out onto a wire rack.
- Put the sugar in a saucepan with 675 ml / 1 pint 4 fl. oz / 2 ¾ cups water and stir over a medium heat to dissolve the sugar. Boil the sugar water for 5 minutes or until it starts to turn syrupy, then stir in the rum.
- Transfer the baba to a mixing bowl, pour over the syrup and leave to soak until cold, turning occasionally.
- Whip the cream until it holds its shape. Transfer the baba to a serving plate and top with the fruit and quenelles of cream.

Steamed Fruit Cake

SERVES 8

PREPARATION TIME 35 MINUTES, PLUS OVERNIGHT SOAKING

COOKING TIME 3 HOURS

INGREDIENTS

350 g / 12 oz / 1 ¾ cups mixed dried fruit
55 ml / 2 fl. oz / ¼ cup brandy
110 g / 4 oz / ½ cup butter, softened
2 tbsp treacle
110 g / 4 oz / ½ cup dark brown sugar
2 large eggs, beaten
55 g / 2 oz / ⅓ cup self-raising flour
2 tsp mixed spice
1 tbsp ground almonds
pouring cream to serve

METHOD

- Mix the dried fruit with the brandy and leave to macerate overnight.
- Cream the butter, treacle and sugar together until well whipped then gradually whisk in the eggs, beating well after each addition. Sift over the flour and spice and fold in with the ground almonds and dried fruit.
- Scrape the mixture into a large buttered pudding basin. Add a pleated sheet of buttered foil to the top and tie securely with string to make a handle.
- Steam the cake for 3 hours, making sure you check and top up the water if it starts to run low. Leave to stand for 10 minutes, then turn it out onto a plate and serve with cream.

Dundee Cake

SERVES 10

PREPARATION TIME OVERNIGHT

COOKING TIME 1 HOUR 15 MINUTES

INGREDIENTS

350 g / 12 oz / 1 ¾ cups mixed dried fruit
55 g / 2 oz / ¼ cup glacé cherries, quartered
55 ml / 2 fl. oz / ¼ cup whisky
110 g / 4 oz / ½ cup butter, softened
2 tbsp treacle
110 g / 4 oz / ½ cup dark brown sugar
2 large eggs, beaten
55 g / 2 oz / ⅓ cup self-raising flour
2 tsp mixed spice
1 tbsp ground almonds
brazil nuts, walnuts and macadamia nuts to decorate
3 tbsp marmalade
1 tbsp whisky

METHOD

- Mix the dried fruit and cherries together and pour over the whisky. Leave to macerate overnight.
- Preheat the oven to 150°C (130°C fan) / 300F / gas 2 and grease and line a 20 cm (8 in) square cake tin with greaseproof paper.
- Cream the butter, treacle and sugar together until well whipped then gradually whisk in the eggs, beating well after each addition. Sift over the flour and spice and fold it in with the ground almonds and dried fruit.
- Scrape the mixture into the tin and arrange the nuts on top. Bake for 1 hour 15 minutes or until a skewer inserted in the centre comes out clean. Turn the loaf out onto a wire rack and leave to cool.
- Heat the marmalade and whisky together, then pass it through a sieve to remove the peel and brush it over the top of the cake to glaze.

Glazed Raspberry Financiers

MAKES 12

PREPARATION TIME 1 HOUR 30 MINUTES

COOKING TIME 10–15 MINUTES

INGREDIENTS

110 g / 4 oz / ½ cup butter
55 g / 2 oz / ⅓ cup plain (all purpose) flour
55 g / 2 oz / ½ cup ground almonds
110 g / 4 oz / 1 cup icing (confectioners') sugar
3 large egg whites
100 g / 3 ½ oz / ⅔ cup raspberries
100 g / 1 ¾ oz / ½ cup raspberry jelly (jello) cubes

METHOD

- Preheat the oven to 170°C (150°C fan) / 325F / gas 3 and oil and flour a 12-hole financier mould.
- Heat the butter until it foams and starts to smell nutty then leave to cool. Combine the flour, ground almonds and icing sugar in a bowl and whisk in the egg whites. Pour the cooled butter through a sieve into the bowl and whisk into the mixture until evenly mixed.
- Spoon the mixture into the moulds and press a few raspberries into each one, then transfer the tin to the oven and bake for 10–15 minutes. Test with a wooden toothpick, if it comes out clean, the cakes are done. Transfer the cakes to a wire rack and leave to cool.
- Make up the jelly according to the packet instructions, using half the recommended amount of water. Leave to cool at room temperature until it just starts to gel, then spoon the mixture onto the cakes to glaze.

Lemon Sponge Cake

SERVES 8

PREPARATION TIME 15 MINUTES

COOKING TIME 40 MINUTES

INGREDIENTS

175 g / 6 oz / 1 ¼ cups self-raising flour, sifted
1 tsp baking powder
175 g / 6 oz / ¾ cup caster (superfine) sugar
175 g / 6 oz / ¾ cup butter, softened
3 large eggs
2 lemons, zest finely grated

METHOD

- Preheat the oven to 180°C (160°C fan) / 350F / gas 4 and oil and line a 23 cm (9 in) round cake tin with greaseproof paper.
- Combine the flour, baking powder, sugar, butter, eggs and lemon zest in a bowl and whisk together for 2 minutes or until smooth.
- Scrape the mixture into the tin and level the top then bake for 40 minutes or until a toothpick inserted in the centre comes out clean. Turn the cake out onto a wire rack and leave to cool completely.

Fruit and Almond Loaf Cake

SERVES 8

PREPARATION TIME 15 MINUTES

COOKING TIME 55 MINUTES

INGREDIENTS

225 g / 8 oz / 1 ½ cups self-raising flour
100 g / 3 ½ oz / ½ cup butter, cubed
85 g / 3 oz / ⅓ cup caster (superfine) sugar
150 g / 5 ½ oz / ¾ cup mixed dried fruit
1 large egg
75 ml / 2 ½ fl. oz / ⅓ cup whole milk
75 g / 2 ½ oz / 1 cup blanched almonds

METHOD

- Preheat the oven to 180°C (160°C fan) / 355F / gas 4 and line a loaf tin with non-stick baking paper.
- Sieve the flour into a mixing bowl and rub in the butter until it resembles fine breadcrumbs then stir in the sugar and dried fruit. Lightly beat the egg with the milk and stir it into the dry ingredients until just combined.
- Scrape the mixture into the loaf tin and sprinkle over the almonds. Bake for 55 minutes or until a skewer inserted in the centre comes out clean. Transfer the cake to a wire rack and leave to cool completely.

Decorated Marble Loaf Cake

SERVES 8

PREPARATION TIME 30 MINUTES

COOKING TIME 45–50 MINUTES

INGREDIENTS

100 g / 3 ½ oz / ⅔ cup self-raising flour
1 tsp baking powder
50 g / 1 ¾ oz / ½ cup ground almonds
150 g / 5 ½ oz / ⅔ cup caster (superfine) sugar
150 g / 5 ½ oz / ⅔ cup butter, softened
3 large eggs
2 tbsp unsweetened cocoa powder

FOR THE TOPPING

200 ml / 7 fl. oz / ¾ cup double (heavy) cream
200 g / 7 oz / 1 ¼ cups dark chocolate, minimum 60% cocoa solids, chopped
chocolate balls, cornflakes and chocolate cornflakes to decorate

METHOD

- Preheat the oven to 180°C (160°C fan) / 350F / gas 4 and grease and line a loaf tin with greaseproof paper.
- Sieve the flour and baking powder into a mixing bowl then add the ground almonds, sugar, butter and eggs and whisk with an electric whisk for 4 minutes or until pale and well whipped.
- Divide the mixture into 2 bowls. Mix the cocoa powder with 2 tbsp hot water until smooth and stir it into one of the bowls. Spoon the mixtures into the tin, alternating between chocolate and plain, then draw a knife through the middle to marble.
- Bake for 45–50 minutes. Insert a toothpick into the centre, if it comes out clean the cake is done. Transfer the cake to a wire rack to cool completely.
- Heat the cream until it starts to simmer, then pour it over the chopped chocolate and stir until smooth. Leave to thicken a little, then spoon it over the cake and top with chocolate balls, cornflakes and chocolate cornflakes.

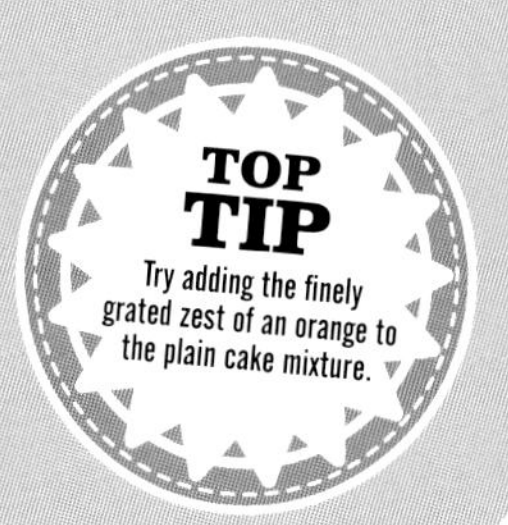

Black Forest Gateau

SERVES 10

PREPARATION TIME 1 HOUR

COOKING TIME 25–30 MINUTES

INGREDIENTS

200 g / 7 oz / 1 ⅓ cups self-raising flour
200 g / 7 oz / ¾ cup caster (superfine) sugar
200 g / 7 oz / ¾ cup butter
4 large eggs
1 tsp baking powder
3 tbsp unsweetened cocoa powder

FOR THE FILLING

250 g / 9 oz / 1 ⅔ cups black cherries, stoned
4 tbsp caster (superfine) sugar
2 tbsp kirsch
300 g / 10 ½ fl. oz / 1 ¼ cups double (heavy) cream

FOR THE TOPPING

200 ml / 7 fl. oz / ¾ cup double (heavy) cream
200 g / 7 oz / 1 ¼ cups dark chocolate, minimum 60% cocoa solids, chopped
2 tbsp chocolate flakes
3 whole cherries, stalks intact
2 tbsp icing (confectioners') sugar, plus extra for dusting

METHOD

- Preheat the oven to 180°C (160°C fan) / 350F / gas 4 and grease and line two 20 cm (8 in) round loose-bottomed cake tins.
- Put all of the cake ingredients in a large mixing bowl and whisk with an electric whisk for 4 minutes or until pale and well whipped. Divide the mixture between the tins and level the tops with a spatula then bake for 25–30 minutes. The cakes are ready when a toothpick inserted in the centre comes out clean. Leave to cool completely.
- Put the cherries in a saucepan with the sugar and kirsch, then cover and cook for 10 minutes or until soft. Leave to cool completely.
- Whip the cream until it holds its shape. Strain the cherries and brush the juice over the cakes. Spread half of the cream on top of one of the cakes and top with the cherries. Top with the other cake and coat the top and sides with the rest of the cream.
- Heat the cream to simmering point, then pour it over the chocolate. Wait for 30 seconds, then stir until smoothly combined. Pour the ganache over the cake, allowing it to drip down the sides. Sprinkle with chocolate flakes.
- Stir a few drops of water into the icing sugar to make a pourable icing, then dip in the cherries. Transfer to the top of the cake and leave to set. Dust the cake with icing sugar just before serving.

Chocolate Sponge Cake

SERVES 8

PREPARATION TIME 20 MINUTES

COOKING TIME 35 MINUTES

INGREDIENTS

175 g / 6 oz / 1 ¼ cups self-raising flour
175 g / 6 oz / ¾ cup caster (superfine) sugar
175 g / 6 oz / ¾ cup butter, softened
3 large eggs
1 tsp baking powder
3 tbsp unsweetened cocoa powder
8 raspberries, plus extra to serve
icing (confectioners') sugar for dusting

METHOD

- Preheat the oven to 180°C (160°C fan) / 350F / gas 4 and grease and line a 23 cm (9 in) round loose-bottomed cake tin.
- Put the flour, sugar, butter, eggs, baking powder and cocoa in a large mixing bowl and whisk with an electric whisk for 4 minutes or until pale and well whipped.
- Scrape the mixture into the tin and level the top with a spatula. Bake for 35 minutes or until a toothpick inserted in the centre comes out clean. Transfer the cake to a wire rack and leave to cool completely.
- Arrange the raspberries on top of the cake and dust lightly with icing sugar.

Biscuits and Cookies

Almond Biscuits

MAKES 36

PREPARATION TIME 1 HOUR

COOKING TIME 25 MINUTES

INGREDIENTS

75 g / 2 ½ oz / ⅓ cup caster (superfine) sugar
175 g / 6 oz / ¾ cup butter, softened
150 g / 5 ½ oz / 1 cup plain (all purpose) flour
150 g / 5 ½ oz / 1 ½ cups ground almonds

METHOD

- Cream together the sugar and butter until pale and well whipped then stir in the flour and ground almonds. Bring the mixture together into a ball with your hands then wrap in cling film and refrigerate for 45 minutes.
- Preheat the oven to 140°C (120°C fan) / 275F / gas 1 and line 2 baking sheets with greaseproof paper.
- Divide the dough into 36 evenly sized balls, then flatten them onto the prepared trays.
- Bake the biscuits for 25 minutes or until cooked through and golden. Transfer the biscuits to a wire rack and leave to cool completely.

Ginger Nuts

MAKES 36

PREPARATION TIME 10 MINUTES

COOKING TIME 15 MINUTES

INGREDIENTS

75 g / 2 ½ oz / ⅓ cup butter, softened
100 g / 3 ½ oz / ⅓ cup golden syrup
225 g / 8 oz / 1 ½ cups self-raising flour
100 g / 3 ½ oz / ½ cup caster (superfine) sugar
2 tsp ground ginger
1 large egg, beaten

METHOD

- Preheat the oven to 180°C (160°C fan) / 355F / gas 4 and line 2 baking sheets with greaseproof paper.
- Melt the butter and golden syrup together in a saucepan. Mix the flour, sugar and ground ginger together then stir in the melted butter mixture and the beaten egg.
- Use a teaspoon to portion the mixture onto the baking trays, leaving plenty of room for the biscuits to spread.
- Bake for 15 minutes or until golden brown. Transfer the biscuits to a wire rack and leave to cool and harden.

Sugar Nib Shortbread

MAKES 16

PREPARATION TIME 20 MINUTES

COOKING TIME 15–20 MINUTES

INGREDIENTS

225 g / 8 oz / 1 ½ cups plain (all purpose) flour
75 g / 2 ½ oz / ⅓ cup caster (superfine) sugar
150 g / 5 oz / ⅔ cup butter, cubed
50 g / 1 ¾ oz / ¼ cup sugar nibs

METHOD

- Preheat the oven to 180°C (160°C fan) / 355F / gas 4 and line a baking tray with greaseproof paper.
- Mix together the flour and caster sugar in a bowl, then rub in the butter. Knead gently until the mixture forms a smooth dough then form into a cylinder 6 cm (2 ½ in) in diameter.
- Slice the roll into 1 cm (½ in) thick slices and spread them out on the baking tray then sprinkle over the sugar nibs and press down lightly.
- Bake the biscuits for 15–20 minutes, turning the tray round halfway through. Transfer the biscuits to a wire rack and leave to cool.

Ginger Crunch Cookies

MAKES 24

PREPARATION TIME 1 HOUR

COOKING TIME 15 MINUTES

INGREDIENTS

100 g / 3 ½ oz / ½ cup caster (superfine) sugar

100 g / 3 ½ oz ⅓ cup butter, softened

3 tsp ground ginger

1 large egg, beaten

300 g / 10 ½ oz / 2 cups plain (all purpose) flour

METHOD

- Cream together the sugar, butter and ground ginger until pale and well whipped then beat in the egg, followed by the flour.
- Bring the mixture together into a ball with your hands then wrap in cling film and refrigerate for 45 minutes.
- Preheat the oven to 190°C (170°C fan) / 375F / gas 5 and line 2 baking sheets with greaseproof paper.
- Divide the dough into 24 pieces and roll into balls. Flatten them slightly onto the prepared baking trays then bake for 15 minutes or until cooked through and golden brown. Transfer the biscuits to a wire rack and leave to cool completely.

Sponge Finger Biscuits

MAKES 45–50

PREPARATION TIME 20 MINUTES

COOKING TIME 10–15 MINUTES

INGREDIENTS

4 large eggs
125 g / 4 ½ oz / ½ cup caster (superfine) sugar
1 tsp vanilla extract
a pinch cream of tartar
110 g / 4 oz / ⅔ cup plain (all purpose) flour
icing (confectioners') sugar for dusting

METHOD

- Preheat the oven to 190°C (170°C fan) / 375F / gas 5 and grease and line 2 large baking trays with greaseproof paper.
- Separate the eggs and put the yolks in a bowl with half of the sugar and the vanilla extract. Whisk for 4 minutes or until very thick and pale.
- Whisk the egg whites with the cream of tartar, making sure the whisk and bowl are completely clean and grease-free. When the egg white reaches the soft peak stage, gradually whisk in the remaining sugar.
- Sieve the flour over the egg yolk mixture and scrape in the egg whites, then carefully fold it all together with a large metal spoon, retaining as much air as possible.
- Spoon the mixture into a piping bag fitted with a large plain nozzle. Pipe 10 cm (4 in) lines onto the baking trays, leaving room for the biscuits to spread. Bake the biscuits for 10–15 minutes or until firm to the touch.
- Transfer to a wire rack and leave to cool completely then dust liberally with icing sugar.

Sugared Pastry Diamonds

MAKES 36

PREPARATION TIME 45 MINUTES

COOKING TIME 10 MINUTES

INGREDIENTS

100 g / 3 ½ oz / ½ cup butter, cubed and chilled
200 g / 7 oz / 1 ⅓ cups plain (all purpose) flour
1 egg, beaten
3 tbsp granulated sugar

METHOD

- Rub the butter into the flour until the mixture resembles fine breadcrumbs. Stir in just enough cold water to bring the pastry together into a pliable dough then chill for 30 minutes.
- Preheat the oven to 200°C (180°C fan) / 390F / gas 6.
- Roll out the pastry on a floured surface then brush the surface with egg and sprinkle with sugar. Use a fluted pastry wheel to cut the sheet into diamonds, then transfer them to a non-stick baking tray.
- Bake the pastry for 10 minutes or until golden brown and crisp. Transfer to a wire rack and leave to cool before serving.

Chocolate Chip Cookies

MAKES 36

PREPARATION TIME 10 MINUTES

COOKING TIME 15 MINUTES

INGREDIENTS

225 g / 8 oz / 1 ⅓ cups light brown sugar
100 g / 3 ½ oz / ½ cup caster (superfine) sugar
175 g / 6 oz / ¾ cup butter, melted
2 tsp vanilla extract
1 egg, plus 1 egg yolk
250 g / 9 oz / 1 ⅔ cups self-raising flour
100 g / 3 ½ oz / ⅔ cup milk chocolate chips

METHOD

- Preheat the oven to 160°C (140°C fan) / 325F / gas 3 and line 2 baking sheets with greaseproof paper.
- Cream together the two sugars, butter and vanilla extract until pale and well whipped then beat in the egg and yolk, followed by the flour and chocolate chips.
- Drop tablespoons of the mixture onto the prepared trays, leaving plenty of room to spread.
- Bake the cookies in batches for 15 minutes or until the edges are starting to brown, but the centres are still chewy. Transfer to a wire rack and leave to cool.

Chocolate Chip Shortbread

MAKES **16**

PREPARATION TIME **20 MINUTES**

COOKING TIME **15–20 MINUTES**

INGREDIENTS

225 g / 8 oz / 1 ½ cups plain (all purpose) flour
75 g / 2 ½ oz / / ⅓ cup caster (superfine) sugar
150 g / 5 oz / ⅔ cup butter, cubed
50 g / 1 ¾ oz / ¼ cup chocolate chips
2 tbsp unsweetened cocoa powder

METHOD

- Preheat the oven to 180°C (160°C fan) / 355F / gas 4 and line a baking tray with greaseproof paper.
- Mix together the flour and caster sugar in a bowl, then rub in the butter. Knead gently with the chocolate chips until the mixture forms a smooth dough then form into a cylinder 6 cm (2 ⅓ in) in diameter.
- Roll the cylinder in cocoa, then cut the roll into 1 cm (½ in) thick slices and spread them out on the baking tray.
- Bake the biscuits for 15–20 minutes, turning the tray round halfway through. Transfer the biscuits to a wire rack and leave to cool.

Glazed Lemon Madeleines

MAKES 12

PREPARATION TIME 1 HOUR 45 MINUTES

COOKING TIME 10–15 MINUTES

INGREDIENTS

110 g / 4 oz / ½ cup butter
55 g / 2 oz / ⅓ cup plain (all purpose) flour
1 lemon, zest finely grated
55 g / 2 oz / ½ cup ground almonds
110 g / 4 oz / 1 cup icing (confectioners') sugar
3 large egg whites

FOR THE GLAZE

1 lemon, juiced
110 g / 4 oz / 1 cup icing (confectioners') sugar

METHOD

- Heat the butter until it foams and starts to smell nutty then leave to cool.
- Combine the flour, lemon zest, ground almonds and icing sugar in a bowl and whisk in the eggs whites. Pour the cooled butter through a sieve into the bowl and whisk into the mixture until evenly mixed. Leave the cake mixture to rest in the fridge for an hour.
- Preheat the oven to 170°C (150°C fan) / 325F / gas 3 and oil and flour a 12-hole madeleine mould.
- Spoon the mixture into the moulds, then transfer the tin to the oven and bake for 10–15 minutes. Test with a wooden toothpick, if it comes out clean, the cakes are done. Transfer the cakes to a wire rack to cool.
- To make the glaze, stir the lemon juice into the icing sugar a little at a time until it forms a pourable icing. Dip the Madeleines in the icing to coat, then leave to dry and set on a wire rack.

Chocolate and Brazil Nut Cookies

MAKES 36

PREPARATION TIME 30 MINUTES

COOKING TIME 15 MINUTES

INGREDIENTS

225 g / 8 oz / 1 ⅓ cups light brown sugar
100 g / 3 ½ oz / ½ cup caster (superfine) sugar
175 g / 6 oz / ¾ cup butter, melted
2 tsp vanilla extract
1 egg, plus 1 egg yolk
250 g / 9 oz / 1 ⅔ cups self-raising flour
100 g / 3 ½ oz / ⅔ cup milk chocolate chips
50 g / 1 ¾ oz / ½ cup brazil nuts, chopped
100 g / 3 ½ oz milk chocolate, broken into squares

METHOD

- Preheat the oven to 160°C (140°C fan) / 325F / gas 3 and line 2 baking sheets with greaseproof paper.
- Cream together the two sugars, butter and vanilla extract until pale and well whipped then beat in the egg and yolk, followed by the flour, chocolate chips and brazil nuts.
- Drop tablespoons of the mixture onto the prepared trays, leaving plenty of room to spread.
- Bake the cookies in batches for 15 minutes or until the edges are starting to brown, but the centres are still chewy. Transfer to a wire rack and leave to cool.
- Melt the chocolate in a microwave or bain marie, then dip the underside of each biscuit and leave to set on greaseproof paper.

Chocolate Chip and Almond Cookies

MAKES 36

PREPARATION TIME 10 MINUTES

COOKING TIME 15 MINUTES

INGREDIENTS

225 g / 8 oz / 1 ⅓ cups light brown sugar
100 g / 3 ½ oz / ½ cup caster (superfine) sugar
175 g / 6 oz / ¾ cup butter, melted
1 tsp almond extract
1 egg, plus 1 egg yolk
250 g / 9 oz / 1 ⅔ cups self-raising flour
50 g / 1 ¾ oz / ⅔ cup flaked (slivered) almonds, chopped
100 g / 3 ½ oz / ⅔ cup milk chocolate chips

METHOD

- Preheat the oven to 160°C (140°C fan) / 325F / gas 3 and line 2 baking sheets with greaseproof paper.
- Cream together the two sugars, butter and almond extract until pale and well whipped then beat in the egg and yolk, followed by the flour, almonds and chocolate chips.
- Drop tablespoons of the mixture onto the prepared trays, leaving plenty of room to spread.
- Bake the cookies in batches for 15 minutes or until the edges are starting to brown, but the centres are still chewy. Transfer to a wire rack and leave to cool.

Jam Flower Biscuits

MAKES 36

PREPARATION TIME 1 HOUR 15 MINUTES

COOKING TIME 25 MINUTES

INGREDIENTS

150 g / 5 ½ oz / ⅔ cup caster (superfine) sugar
350 g / 12 oz / 1 ½ cups butter, softened
1 tsp vanilla extract
300 g / 10 ½ oz / 2 cups plain (all purpose) flour
150 g / 5 ½ oz / 1 ½ cups ground almonds
125 g / 4 ½ oz / ½ cup strawberry jam (jelly)
125 g / 4 ½ oz / ½ cup apricot jam (jelly)

METHOD

- Cream together the sugar, butter and vanilla extract until pale and well whipped then stir in the flour and ground almonds. Bring the mixture together into a ball with your hands then wrap in cling film and refrigerate for 45 minutes.
- Preheat the oven to 140°C (120°C fan) / 275F / gas 1 and line 2 baking sheets with greaseproof paper.
- Roll out the dough on a lightly floured surface to 5 mm (¼ in) thick. Use a flower-shaped pastry cutter to cut out 72 biscuits, re-rolling the trimmings as necessary. Use a small round cutter to cut out the centre of 36 of the biscuits.
- Transfer the biscuits to the prepared trays and bake in batches for 25 minutes or until cooked through and golden. Transfer the biscuits to a wire rack and leave to cool completely.
- Sandwich the plain biscuits and centre-less biscuits together in pairs with the jam.

Peppermint Sponge Fingers

MAKES 45–50
PREPARATION TIME 20 MINUTES
COOKING TIME 10–15 MINUTES

INGREDIENTS

4 large eggs
125 g / 4 ½ oz / ½ cup caster (superfine) sugar
a few drops of peppermint essence
a pinch cream of tartar
110 g / 4 oz / ⅔ cup plain (all purpose) flour
icing (confectioners') sugar for dusting
mint-choc-chip ice cream and peppermint tea to serve

METHOD

- Preheat the oven to 190°C (170°C fan) / 375F / gas 5 and grease and line 2 large baking trays with greaseproof paper.
- Separate the eggs and put the yolks in a bowl with half of the sugar and the peppermint essence. Whisk for 4 minutes or until very thick and pale.
- Whisk the egg whites with the cream of tartar, making sure the whisk and bowl are completely clean and grease-free. When the egg white reaches the soft peak stage, gradually whisk in the remaining sugar.
- Sieve the flour over the egg yolk mixture and scrape in the egg whites, then carefully fold it all together, retaining as much air as possible.
- Spoon the mixture into a piping bag fitted with a large plain nozzle. Pipe 10 cm (4 in) lines onto the baking trays, leaving room for the biscuits to spread. Bake the biscuits for 10–15 minutes or until firm to the touch.
- Transfer to a wire rack and leave to cool completely then dust liberally with icing sugar. Serve with mint-choc-chip ice cream and peppermint tea.

Double Choc and Nut Cookies

MAKES 36

PREPARATION TIME 30 MINUTES

COOKING TIME 15 MINUTES

INGREDIENTS

225 g / 8 oz / 1 ⅓ cups light brown sugar
100 g / 3 ½ oz / ½ cup caster (superfine) sugar
175 g / 6 oz / ¾ cup butter, melted
2 tsp vanilla extract
1 egg, plus 1 egg yolk
200 g / 7 oz / 1 ⅓ cups self-raising flour
50 g / ⅓ oz / ½ cup unsweetened cocoa powder
100 g / 3 ½ oz / ⅔ cup dark chocolate chips
50 g / 1 ¾ oz / ½ cup peanuts, chopped

METHOD

- Preheat the oven to 160°C (140°C fan) / 325F / gas 3 and line 2 baking sheets with greaseproof paper.
- Cream together the two sugars, butter and vanilla extract until pale and well whipped then beat in the egg and yolk, followed by the flour, cocoa, chocolate chips and peanuts.
- Drop tablespoons of the mixture onto the prepared trays, leaving plenty of room to spread.
- Bake the cookies in batches for 15 minutes or until the edges are starting to brown, but the centres are still chewy. Transfer to a wire rack and leave to cool.

Chocolate Sandwich Biscuits

MAKES 24

PREPARATION TIME 1 HOUR 15 MINUTES

COOKING TIME 25 MINUTES

INGREDIENTS

150 g / 5 ½ oz / ⅔ cup caster (superfine) sugar
350 g / 12 oz / 1 ½ cups butter, softened
300 g / 10 ½ oz / 2 cups plain (all purpose) flour
150 g / 5 ½ oz / 1 ½ cups ground almonds
150 g / 5 ½ oz / 1 cup dark chocolate (minimum 70% cocoa solids)

METHOD

- Cream together the sugar and butter until pale and well whipped then stir in the flour and ground almonds. Bring the mixture together into a ball with your hands then wrap in cling film and refrigerate for 45 minutes.
- Preheat the oven to 140°C (120°C fan) / 275F / gas 1 and line 2 baking sheets with greaseproof paper.
- Roll out the dough on a lightly floured surface to 5 mm (¼ in) thick. Use a round fluted pastry cutter to cut out 48 biscuits, rerolling the trimmings as necessary. Use a small, heart-shaped cutter to cut the centre out of 24 of the biscuits.
- Transfer the biscuits to the prepared trays and bake in batches for 25 minutes or until cooked through and golden. Transfer the biscuits to a wire rack and leave to cool completely.
- Melt the chocolate in a microwave or bain marie, then use to sandwich the plain biscuits and centre-less biscuits together in pairs. Allow the chocolate to set before serving.

Demerara Meringues

MAKES 8

PREPARATION TIME 20 MINUTES

COOKING TIME 1 HOUR

INGREDIENTS

4 large egg whites

110g / 4 oz / 1 cup caster (superfine) sugar

2 tbsp demerara sugar

METHOD

- Preheat the oven to 140°C (120°C fan) / 275F / gas 1 and oil and line a large baking tray with greaseproof paper.
- Whisk the egg whites until stiff, then gradually whisk in half the caster sugar until the mixture is very shiny. Fold in the remaining caster sugar with a large metal spoon, being careful to retain as much air as possible.
- Spoon the meringue into a piping bag fitted with a large star nozzle and pipe 8 swirls onto the baking tray. Sprinkle the tops with demerara sugar, then transfer the tray to the oven and bake for 1 hour.
- Turn off the oven and leave the meringues to cool slowly inside before serving.

Raspberry Macaroons

MAKES 18

PREPARATION TIME 1 HOUR 15 MINUTES

COOKING TIME 10–15 MINUTES

INGREDIENTS

175 g / 6 oz / 1 ½ cups ground almonds
175 g / 6 oz / 1 ½ cups icing (confectioners') sugar
2 large egg whites
1 tbsp raspberry syrup
a few drops of pink food dye
110 g / 4 oz / ½ cup raspberry jam (jelly)

METHOD

- Oil and line a large baking sheet with baking parchment.
- Grind the ground almonds and icing sugar together in a food processor to a very fine powder. Whisk the egg whites to stiff peaks in a very clean bowl then carefully fold in the almond and sugar mixture with the raspberry syrup and food dye.
- Spoon the mixture into a piping bag fitted with a large plain nozzle and pipe 2.5 cm (1 in) rounds onto the baking tray. Leave the uncooked macaroons to stand for 30 minutes to form a skin.
- Preheat the oven to 170°C (150°C fan) / 325F / gas 3.
- Bake for 10–15 minutes or until crisp on the outside and still a bit chewy in the middle. Slide the greaseproof paper onto a cold work surface and leave the macaroons to cool completely. Sandwich the macaroons together with jam.

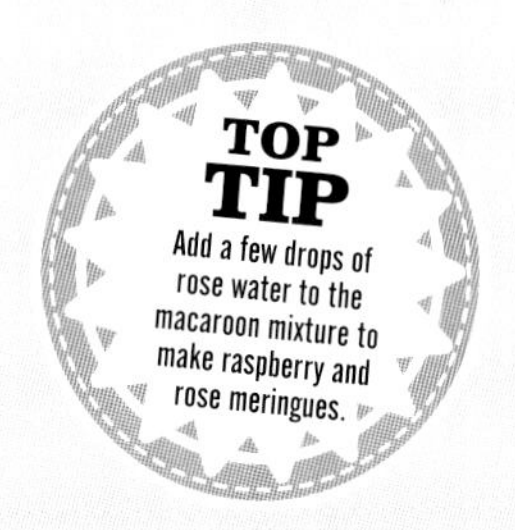

Desserts

Rhubarb Meringue Pie

MAKES 4

PREPARATION TIME 10–15 MINUTES

COOKING TIME 20–25 MINUTES

INGREDIENTS

250 g / 9 oz ready-made shortcrust pastry
a little plain (all purpose) flour, for dusting
675 g / 1 lb 8 oz / 5 cups rhubarb, trimmed and sliced
75 g / 3 oz / ⅓ cup caster (superfine) sugar
60 ml / 2 fl. oz / ¼ cup cold water

FOR THE MERINGUE

2 medium egg whites
110 g / 4 oz / ½ cup caster (superfine) sugar
¼ tsp cream of tartar
a pinch of salt

TO GARNISH

1 tbsp icing (confectioners') sugar

METHOD

- Preheat the oven to 180°C (160°C fan) / 350F / gas 4.
- Roll the pastry out on a lightly floured surface to 5 mm (¼ in) thickness. Cut out 4 rounds of pastry and use to line 4 individual 12 cm (5 in) fluted tartlet cases.
- Prick the bases with a fork and trim any excess, overhanging pastry.
- Line with greaseproof paper and fill with baking beans before blind-baking for 12–15 minutes until golden at the edges.
- Remove from the oven, discard the greaseproof paper and baking beans then return to the oven for 3–4 minutes to brown the base. Remove to a wire rack to cool.
- Combine the rhubarb, sugar and water in a saucepan and cook over a medium heat, covered, until soft. Drain and cool to one side.
- Whisk the egg whites with the salt in a large, clean mixing bowl until soft peaks form.
- Add the cream of tartar and the sugar, 1 tablespoon at at time, beating well between additions until you have a thick, glossy meringue. Spoon into a piping bag fitted with a 2 cm (1 in) star-shaped nozzle.
- Increase the oven to 220°C (200°C fan) / 425F / gas 7. Fill the pastry with the rhubarb and pipe the meringue on top in blobs.
- Bake for 8–10 minutes until the meringue is browned, then remove from the oven. Dust with icing sugar before serving.

Summer Fruit Crumble

SERVES **4**

PREPARATION TIME **10 MINUTES**

COOKING TIME **40 MINUTES**

INGREDIENTS

300 g / 10 ½ oz / 2 cups mixed summer fruit
4 tbsp caster (superfine) sugar
75 g / 2 ½ oz / ⅓ cup butter
50 g / 1 ¾ oz / ⅓ cup plain (all purpose) flour
25 g / 1 oz / ½ cup ground almonds
40 g / 1 ½ oz / ¼ cup light brown sugar

METHOD

- Preheat the oven to 180°C (160°C fan) / 355F / gas 4.
- Mix the fruit with the caster sugar and tip it into a baking dish.
- Rub the butter into the flour and stir in the ground almonds and brown sugar. Take a handful of the topping and squeeze it into a clump, then crumble it over the fruit.
- Repeat with the rest of the crumble mixture then bake for 40 minutes or until the topping is golden brown.

Lemon Curd Tart

SERVES 8

PREPARATION TIME 55 MINUTES

COOKING TIME 15–20 MINUTES

INGREDIENTS

2 tsp cornflour (cornstarch)
4 lemons, zested and juiced
4 large eggs, beaten
225 g / 8 oz / 1 cup butter
175 g / 6 oz / ¾ cup caster (superfine) sugar

FOR THE PASTRY

100 g / 3 ½ oz / ½ cup butter, cubed
200 g / 7 oz / 1 ⅓ cups plain (all purpose) flour
55 g / 2 oz / ½ cup caster (superfine) sugar
1 egg, beaten

TO DECORATE

1 lemon, zest finely pared
2 slices lemon

METHOD

- Preheat the oven to 200°C (180°C fan) / 390F / gas 6.
- To make the pastry, rub the butter into the flour and sugar then add the egg with just enough cold water to bind. Wrap the dough in cling film and chill for 30 minutes, then roll out on a floured surface.
- Use the pastry to line a 23 cm (9 in) loose-bottomed tart tin and trim the edges. Prick the pastry with a fork, line with cling film and fill with baking beans or rice. Bake for 10 minutes then remove the cling film and baking beans and cook for another 8 minutes to crisp.
- Meanwhile, dissolve the cornflour in the lemon juice and put it in a saucepan with the rest of the ingredients. Stir constantly over a medium heat to melt the butter and dissolve the sugar. After 6 or 7 minutes the mixture should thicken. Continue until it starts to bubble then spoon it into the pastry case and level with a palette knife.
- Leave to cool completely before decorating with the lemon zest and slices.

Strawberry Tartlets

MAKES **6**

PREPARATION TIME **2 HOURS**

COOKING TIME **12 MINUTES**

INGREDIENTS

225 g / 8 oz / 1 ½ cups plain (all purpose) flour
110 g / 4 oz / ½ cup butter, cubed and chilled

FOR THE CRÈME PATISSIERE

2 large egg yolks
55 g / 2 oz / ¼ cup caster (superfine) sugar
2 tbsp plain (all purpose) flour
2 tbsp cornflour (cornstarch)
1 tsp vanilla extract
250 ml / 9 fl. oz / 1 cup milk

TO DECORATE

250 g / 9 oz / 1 ⅔ cups strawberries, quartered
icing (confectioners') sugar for dusting
mint leaves to garnish

METHOD

- Preheat the oven to 200°C (180°C fan) / 400F / gas 6.
- Sieve the flour into a mixing bowl then rub in the butter until the mixture resembles fine breadcrumbs. Stir in just enough cold water to bring the pastry together into a pliable dough.
- Roll out the pastry on a floured surface and cut out 6 circles then use them to line 6 tartlet tins. Line the tins with cling film and fill with baking beans then bake for 10 minutes. Remove the film and beans and return the cases to the oven for 2 minutes or until cooked through. Leave to cool.
- Heat the milk in a saucepan until just simmering. Meanwhile, whisk together the egg yolks, sugar, flours and vanilla in a heatproof bowl. Slowly pour on the milk, whisking all the time, then transfer back to the pan. Heat very gently, stirring constantly, until thickened. Spoon into the pastry cases and leave to cool.
- Pile the strawberries on top of the tartlets and dust with icing sugar. Garnish with mint.

Blueberry Lattice Tartlets

MAKES 4
PREPARATION TIME 1 HOUR
COOKING TIME 25 MINUTES

INGREDIENTS

225 g / 8 oz / 1 ½ cups plain (all purpose) flour
110 g / 4 oz / ½ cup butter, cubed and chilled
150 g / 5 ½ oz / 1 cup blueberries
225 g / 8 oz / 1 cup blueberry jam (jelly)
1 egg, beaten

METHOD

- Preheat the oven to 200°C (180°C fan) / 400F / gas 6.
- Sieve the flour into a mixing bowl then rub in the butter until the mixture resembles fine breadcrumbs. Stir in just enough cold water to bring the pastry together into a pliable dough. Chill for 30 minutes.
- Roll out the pastry on a floured surface and cut out 6 circles then use them to line 6 tartlet tins. Re-roll the trimmings and cut the sheet into 1 cm (½ in) strips.
- Mix the blueberries with the jam and spoon it into the pastry cases. Lay the pastry strips over the top in a lattice pattern and crimp the edges to seal. Brush the pastry with beaten egg.
- Bake the tartlets for 25 minutes or until the pastry is cooked underneath and golden brown on top.

Apple, Almond and Sultana Strudel

SERVES 8

PREPARATION TIME 25 MINUTES

COOKING TIME 35–45 MINUTES

INGREDIENTS

225 g / 8 oz filo / ¾ cup pastry
100 g / 3 ½ oz / ½ cup butter, melted
2 Bramley apples, peeled, cored and chopped
100 g / 3 ½ oz / 1 cup ground almonds
100 g / 3 ½ oz / ⅔ cup golden sultanas
100 g / 3 ½ oz / ½ cup light brown sugar
1 tsp ground cinnamon
2 tbsp flaked (slivered) almonds
icing (confectioners') sugar to dust

METHOD

- Preheat the oven to 180°C (160°C fan) / 355F / gas 4 and grease a large baking tray.
- Brush the filo pastry sheets with melted butter and lay them out on a sheet of cling film so that the square is at least 4 sheets thick.
- Mix the apples with the ground almonds and sultanas and stir in the sugar and cinnamon. Spread the filling out along one edge of the pastry then use the cling film to help you roll it up, tucking in the edges as you go.
- Transfer the strudel to the baking tray, then brush with a little more melted butter and sprinkle with flaked almonds. Bake the strudel in the oven for 35–45 minutes or until the pastry is golden and crisp.
- Dust the strudel with icing sugar before serving.

Pomegranate Cheesecake

SERVES 8

PREPARATION TIME 2 HOURS 40 MINUTES

INGREDIENTS

50 g / 1 ¾ oz / ¼ cup butter

200 g / 7 oz / ¾ cup digestive biscuits, crushed

75 g / 2 ½ oz / ⅔ cup almonds, roughly chopped

150 g / 5 ½ oz / ⅔ cup cream cheese

150 g / 5 ½ oz / ⅔ cup condensed milk

2 lemons, juiced

1 tsp orange flower water

75 g / 2 ½ oz / ⅓ cup pomegranate seeds

METHOD

- Melt the butter and stir in the crushed biscuits and almonds then tip the mixture into a 20 cm (8 in) deep spring-form cake tin and press down well.
- Beat the cream cheese with an electric whisk until smooth then whisk in the condensed milk. Whisk in the lemon juice and orange flower water. When the mixture starts to thicken, scrape it onto the biscuit base and level the top.
- Chill in the fridge for 2 hours or until firm. Un-mould the cheesecake onto a serving plate and top with the pomegranate seeds.

Individual Strawberry Pavlovas

MAKES 4

PREPARATION TIME 1 HOUR 30 MINUTES

COOKING TIME 1 HOUR

INGREDIENTS

4 large egg whites

110 g / 4 oz / 1 cup caster (superfine) sugar

1 tsp cornflour (cornstarch)

225 ml / 8 fl. oz / 1 cup double (heavy) cream

2 tbsp icing (confectioners') sugar

½ tsp vanilla extract

150 g / 5 ½ oz / 1 cup strawberries, halved

4 tbsp strawberry syrup

METHOD

- Preheat the oven to 140°C (120°C fan) / 275F / gas 1 and oil and line a baking tray with greaseproof paper.
- Whisk the egg whites until stiff, then gradually whisk in half the sugar until the mixture is very shiny. Fold in the remaining sugar and the cornflour then spoon the mixture into 4 mounds on the baking tray.
- Bake the meringues for 1 hour or until crisp on the outside, but still a bit chewy in the middle. Turn off the oven and leave to cool completely inside.
- Whip the cream with the icing sugar and vanilla until it just holds its shape, then spoon it on top of the meringues. Arrange the strawberries on top and drizzle with strawberry syrup.

TOP TIP

Replace the strawberries with peach slices and the strawberry syrup with raspberry syrup for peach melba pavlovas.

Apricot Ripple Cheesecake

SERVES 8

PREPARATION TIME 4 HOURS

COOKING TIME 10 MINUTES

INGREDIENTS

12 apricots, halved and stoned
100 ml / 3 ½ fl. oz / ½ cup apple juice
4 tbsp runny honey
50 g / 1 ¾ oz / ¼ cup butter
200 g / 7 oz / ¾ cup digestive biscuits, crushed
150 g / 5 ½ oz / ⅔ cup cream cheese, well chilled
150 g / 5 ½ oz / ⅔ cup condensed milk, well chilled
2 lemons, juiced

METHOD

- Put the apricots in a saucepan with the apple juice and honey. Cover and simmer gently for 8 minutes or until the apricots are soft, then remove from the pan with a slotted spoon and transfer to a liquidiser. Blend with enough of the cooking liquid to make a thick puree, then leave to cool completely.
- Melt the butter and stir in the crushed biscuits, then tip the mixture into a rectangular baking dish and press down firmly into an even layer.
- Beat the cream cheese with an electric whisk until smooth, then whisk in the condensed milk. Whisk in the lemon juice until the mixture starts to thicken, then pour it onto the biscuit base and level the top.
- Spoon dollops of the apricot puree over the top, then swirl the 2 together with a skewer. Chill in the fridge for at least 3 hours before serving.

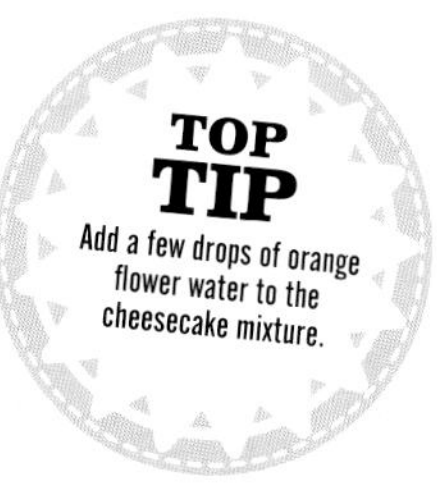

Apple and Thyme Frangipane Tarts

MAKES 6

PREPARATION TIME 20 MINUTES

COOKING TIME 15–20 MINUTES

INGREDIENTS

450 g / 1 lb / 1 ½ cups ready-to-roll puff pastry
75 g / 2 ½ oz / ¾ cup ground almonds
75 g / 2 ½ oz / ⅓ cup butter, softened
75 g / 2 ½ oz / ⅓ cup caster (superfine) sugar
1 large egg
1 tbsp plain (all purpose) flour
½ tbsp thyme leaves
2 eating apples, cored and thinly sliced
thyme sprigs to garnish
icing (confectioners') sugar to dust

METHOD

- Preheat the oven to 200°C (180°C fan) / 400F / gas 6.
- Roll out the pastry on a floured surface and cut out 6 x 10 cm (4 in) circles. Transfer them to a greased baking tray.
- Whisk together the almonds, butter, sugar, eggs, thyme and flour until smoothly whipped, then spoon the mixture onto the pastry circles.
- Arrange a few apple slices on top of each tart, then bake for 15–20 minutes or until the tops are golden brown and the pastry is crisp underneath.
- Serve garnished with thyme and dusted with icing sugar.

Mirabelle Clafoutis

SERVES 6

PREPARATION TIME 20 MINUTES

COOKING TIME 35–45 MINUTES

INGREDIENTS

75 g / 2 ½ oz / ⅓ cup butter
75 g / 2 ½ oz / ⅓ cup caster (superfine) sugar
300 ml / 10 ½ fl. oz / 1 ¼ cups whole milk
2 large eggs
50 g / 1 ¾ oz / ⅓ cup plain (all purpose) flour
2 tbsp ground almonds
300 g / 10 ½ oz / 2 cups mirabelle plums
icing (confectioners') sugar for dusting

METHOD

- Preheat the oven to 190°C (170°C fan) / 375F / gas 5.
- Melt the butter in a saucepan and cook over a low heat until it starts to smell nutty. Brush a little of the butter around the inside of a baking dish then add a spoonful of the caster sugar and shake to coat.
- Whisk together the milk and eggs with the rest of the butter. Sift the flour into a mixing bowl with a pinch of salt, then stir in the ground almonds and the rest of the sugar. Make a well in the middle of the dry ingredients and gradually whisk in the liquid, incorporating all the flour from round the outside until you have a lump-free batter.
- Arrange the mirabelles in the prepared baking dish and pour over the batter. Bake the clafoutis for 35–45 minutes or until a skewer inserted in the centre comes out clean. Dust with icing sugar and serve warm or cold.

Summer Fruit Tartlets

MAKES 6

PREPARATION TIME 2 HOURS

COOKING TIME 12 MINUTES

INGREDIENTS

225 g / 8 oz / 1 ½ cups plain (all purpose) flour

110 g / 4 oz / ½ cup butter, cubed and chilled

FOR THE CRÈME PATISSIERE

2 large egg yolks

55 g / 2 oz / ¼ cup caster (superfine) sugar

2 tbsp plain (all purpose) flour

2 tbsp cornflour (cornstarch)

1 tsp vanilla extract

250 ml / 9 fl. oz / 1 cup whole milk

TO DECORATE

12 strawberries, halved

6 cherries

18 raspberries

icing (confectioners') sugar for dusting

mint leaves to garnish

METHOD

- Preheat the oven to 200°C (180°C fan) / 400F / gas 6.
- Sieve the flour into a mixing bowl then rub in the butter until the mixture resembles fine breadcrumbs. Stir in just enough cold water to bring the pastry together into a pliable dough.
- Heat the milk in a saucepan until just simmering. Meanwhile, whisk together the egg yolks, sugar, flours and vanilla in a heatproof bowl. Slowly pour on the milk, whisking all the time, then transfer back to the pan. Heat very gently, stirring constantly, until thickened. Spoon into the pastry cases and leave to cool.
- To make the crème patissiere, stir the egg yolks, sugar, flours and vanilla extract together in a saucepan, then gradually add the milk. Heat the mixture until it starts to boil, stirring all the time, then take off the heat and beat vigorously to remove any lumps. Spoon the crème patissiere into the tartlet cases and leave to cool.
- Arrange the strawberries, cherries and raspberries on top of the tartlets and dust with icing sugar. Garnish with mint.

Pear Tarte Tatin

SERVES 6

PREPARATION TIME 10 MINUTES

COOKING TIME 40 MINUTES

INGREDIENTS

3 tbsp butter, softened and cubed

5–6 small pears, peeled, quartered and cored

2 star anise

4 tbsp soft light brown sugar

100 ml / 3 ½ fl. oz / ½ cup apple juice

300 g / 10 ½ oz / 1 cup all-butter puff pastry

METHOD

- Preheat the oven to 220°C (200°C fan) / 425F / gas 7.
- Melt the butter in a large frying pan then fry the pears and star anise, in a single layer, for 5 minutes or until they start to brown.
- Stir the sugar into the apple juice and pour it over the pears then cook until the liquid has reduced to a syrupy glaze.
- Arrange the pears in a small oven-proof frying pan and spoon over the cooking liquor.
- Roll out the pastry on a floured surface and cut out a circle the same diameter as the pan.
- Lay the pastry over the pears and tuck in the edges, then transfer the tin to the oven and bake for 25 minutes or until the pastry is golden brown and cooked through.
- Using oven gloves, put a large plate on top of the pan and turn them both over in one smooth movement to un-mould the tart.

Coconut Tart

MAKES 12 SQUARES

PREPARATION TIME 15 MINUTES

COOKING TIME 20 MINUTES

INGREDIENTS

100 g / 3 ½ oz / ½ cup butter, cubed and chilled
200 g / 7 oz / 1 ⅓ cups plain (all purpose) flour
200 g / 7 oz / ⅔ cup raspberry jam (jelly)
2 large egg whites
100 g / 3 ½ oz / ½ cup caster (superfine) sugar
250 g / 9 oz / 1 ¼ cups unsweetened shredded coconut
icing (confectioners') sugar for dusting

METHOD

- Preheat the oven to 200°C (180°C fan) / 400F / gas 6.
- Rub the butter into the flour until the mixture resembles fine breadcrumbs. Stir in just enough cold water to bring the pastry together into a pliable dough, then chill for 30 minutes.
- Roll out the pastry on a floured surface and use it to line a greased Swiss roll tin. Spread the jam on top.
- Whisk the egg whites to stiff peaks in a very clean bowl then fold in the sugar and coconut.
- Spoon the mixture into a piping bag fitted with a large star nozzle and pipe it over the surface in an even layer.
- Bake the tart for 30 minutes or until the pastry is cooked underneath and the coconut topping is golden brown. Leave to cool completely then cut it into 12 squares and dust with icing sugar.

Lemon Domed Biscuits

MAKES 6

PREPARATION TIME 1 HOUR 15 MINUTES

COOKING TIME 20–25 MINUTES

INGREDIENTS

125 g / 4 ½ oz / ½ cup butter, cubed
125 g / 4 ½ oz / ¾ cup plain (all purpose) flour
125 g / 4 ½ oz / ½ cup caster (superfine) sugar
3 large egg yolks, beaten

FOR THE LEMON DOMES

2 tsp cornflour (cornstarch)
4 lemons, zested and juiced
4 large eggs, beaten
225 g / 8 oz / 1 cup butter
175 g / 6 oz / ¾ cup caster (superfine) sugar
4 tbsp icing (confectioners') sugar

METHOD

- Preheat the oven to 180°C (160°C fan) / 350F / gas 4 and line a baking tray with greaseproof paper.
- Rub the butter into the flour with a pinch of salt then stir in the sugar, then stir in the egg yolks. Bring the mixture together into a soft dough and roll it out between 2 sheets of greaseproof paper until 2 cm (¾ in) thick.
- Use a cookie cutter to cut out 6 biscuits and transfer them to a baking tray. Bake the biscuits for 20–25 minutes or until golden brown. Transfer the biscuits to a wire rack and leave to cool.
- Meanwhile, dissolve the cornflour in the lemon juice and put it in a saucepan with the rest of the ingredients except the icing sugar. Stir over a medium heat, after 6 or 7 minutes the mixture should thicken. Continue until it starts to bubble, then spoon it into a 6-hole silicone half-sphere mould. Leave to cool, then chill in the fridge until set.
- Stir cold water into the icing sugar a few drops at a time until you have a thick icing. Spoon it into a piping bag, fitted with a small plain nozzle. Turn each lemon dome out onto a biscuit and drizzle a little icing over the top.

Chocolate and Walnut Fondants

MAKES 6

PREPARATION TIME 50 MINUTES

COOKING TIME 8 MINUTES

INGREDIENTS

2 tbsp walnuts, finely chopped
1 tbsp demerara sugar
150 g / 6 oz / ¾ cup dark chocolate, minimum 60% cocoa solids, chopped
150 g / 6 oz / ⅔ cup butter, chopped
85 g / 3 oz / ⅓ cup caster (superfine) sugar
3 large eggs, plus 3 egg yolks
1 tbsp plain (all purpose) flour
1 tbsp unsweetened cocoa powder

METHOD

- Mix the walnuts and demerara sugar together. Oil the inside of 6 mini pudding basins, then spoon in the walnut mixture and shake to coat.
- Melt the chocolate, butter and caster sugar together in a saucepan, stirring to dissolve the sugar. Leave to cool a little, then beat in the eggs and egg yolks and fold in the flour. Divide the mixture between the pudding basins, then chill for 30 minutes.
- Preheat the oven to 180°C (160°C fan) / 350F / gas 4 and put a baking tray in to heat. Transfer the fondants to the heated baking tray and bake in the oven for 8 minutes.
- Leave the fondants to cool for 2 minutes, then dust with the cocoa powder and serve.

Coconut Soufflés

MAKES 4

PREPARATION TIME 25 MINUTES

COOKING TIME 15–20 MINUTES

INGREDIENTS

3 tbsp desiccated coconut
4 tbsp coconut liqueur
1 tbsp butter, melted
75 g / 2 ½ oz / ⅓ cup caster (superfine) sugar
5 large egg whites
icing (confectioners') sugar for dusting

METHOD

- Preheat the oven to 170°C (150°C fan) / 325F / gas 3 and put a kettle of water on to boil.
- Combine the desiccated coconut and coconut liqueur in a bowl and leave to soften while you prepare the soufflé base.
- Brush 4 large glass ramekins with butter then sprinkle the insides with a tablespoon of the caster sugar.
- Whip the egg whites until they form stiff peaks then gradually whisk in the rest of the caster sugar and beat until thick and shiny. Carefully fold in the coconut mixture, being careful to retain as much air as possible.
- Divide the mixture between the ramekins and level the tops with a palette knife. Run the tip of your thumb round the inside of the dish to create a lip as this will help the soufflés to rise evenly.
- Transfer the ramekins to a roasting tin and pour enough boiling water around them to come halfway up the sides. Bake the soufflés for 15–20 minutes or until they are well risen and a pale golden brown. Dust with icing sugar and serve immediately.

Chocolate Tart

SERVES 8

PREPARATION TIME 35 MINUTES

COOKING TIME 35 MINUTES

INGREDIENTS

225 g / 8 oz / 2 ¼ cups ground almonds
225 g / 8 oz / 1 cup butter, softened
225 g / 8 oz / 1 cup caster (superfine) sugar
3 large eggs
2 tbsp unsweetened cocoa powder, plus extra for dusting
75 g / 2 ½ oz / ½ cup milk chocolate, grated
3 tbsp plain (all purpose) flour
icing (confectioners') sugar for dusting

FOR THE PASTRY

100 g / 3 ½ oz / ½ cup butter, cubed and chilled
200 g / 7 oz / 1 ⅓ cups plain (all purpose) flour
1 egg, beaten
2 tbsp caster (superfine) sugar

METHOD

- First make the pastry. Rub the butter into the flour until the mixture resembles fine breadcrumbs. Stir in just enough cold water to bring the pastry together into a pliable dough then chill for 30 minutes.
- Preheat the oven to 200°C (180°C fan) / 390F / gas 6.
- Roll out the pastry on a floured surface and use it to line a 23 cm (9 in) round tart case. Prick the pastry with a fork, line with cling film and fill with baking beans or rice. Bake for 10 minutes then remove the cling film and baking beans.
- Whisk together the almonds, butter, sugar, eggs, cocoa, chocolate and flour until smoothly whipped, then spoon the mixture into the pastry case.
- Bake the tart for 25 minutes or until the filling is cooked through and the pastry is crisp underneath. Dust the tart with a little cocoa and icing sugar and serve hot or cold.

Jam Tarts with Spiced Pastry

MAKES 6

PREPARATION TIME 1 HOUR

COOKING TIME 25 MINUTES

INGREDIENTS

225 g / 8 oz / 1 ½ cups plain (all purpose) flour
2 tsp mixed spice
110 g / 4 oz / ½ cup butter, cubed and chilled
250 ml / 9 fl. oz / 1 cup strawberry jam (jelly)
1 egg, beaten

METHOD

- Preheat the oven to 200°C (180°C fan) / 400F / gas 6.
- Sieve the flour and spice into a mixing bowl then rub in the butter until the mixture resembles fine breadcrumbs. Stir in just enough cold water to bring the pastry together into a pliable dough. Chill for 30 minutes.
- Roll out the pastry on a floured surface and cut out 6 circles then use them to line 6 tartlet tins. Re-roll the trimmings and cut the sheet into 1 cm (½ in) strips.
- Spoon the jam into the pastry cases, then lay the pastry strips over the top in a lattice pattern and crimp the edges to seal. Brush the pastry with beaten egg.
- Bake the tartlets for 25 minutes or until the pastry is cooked underneath and golden brown on top.

Strawberry and Chocolate Meringue Pie

SERVES 8

PREPARATION TIME 1 HOUR

COOKING TIME 28 MINUTES

INGREDIENTS

100 g / 3 ½ oz / ½ cup butter, cubed
200 g / 7 oz / 1 ⅓ cups plain (all purpose) flour
2 tbsp unsweetened cocoa powder
4 tbsp strawberry jam (jelly)
4 large egg whites
100 g / 3 ½ oz / ½ cup caster (superfine) sugar
150 g / 5 ½ oz / 1 cup strawberries
icing (confectioners') sugar for dusting

METHOD

- Preheat the oven to 200°C (180°C fan) / 390F / gas 6.
- Rub the butter into the flour and cocoa then add just enough cold water to bind. Chill for 30 minutes then roll out on a floured surface. Use the pastry to line a 23 cm (9 in) loose-bottomed tart tin and prick it with a fork.
- Line the pastry with cling film and fill with baking beans or rice then bake for 10 minutes. Remove the cling film and beans and cook for another 8 minutes to crisp. Spoon the jam into the pastry case.
- Whisk the egg whites until stiff, then gradually add the sugar and whisk until the mixture is thick and shiny. Spoon the meringue on top of the jam and smooth with a palette knife. Return to the oven for 10 minutes to lightly brown the top.
- Leave to cool a little, then arrange the strawberries on top and dust with icing sugar.

Apple and Date Filo Pies

MAKES 6

PREPARATION TIME 20 MINUTES

COOKING TIME 20 MINUTES

INGREDIENTS

1 large cooking apple, peeled, cored and diced
3 eating apples, peeled, cored and diced
100 g / 3 ½ oz / ½ cup dates, stoned and chopped
2 tbsp light brown sugar
1 tsp mixed spice
100 g / 3 ½ oz / ½ cup butter
250 g / 9 oz / ¾ cup filo pastry sheets
icing (confectioners') sugar to dust

METHOD

- Preheat the oven to 200°C (180°C fan) / 400F / gas 6.
- Put the apples, dates, sugar and spice in a saucepan with 4 tablespoons of cold water. Put a lid on the pan then cook over a gentle heat for 10 minutes, stirring occasionally.
- Taste the compote and add more sugar if necessary, then divide it between 6 mini casserole dishes.
- Melt the butter then brush it over each filo sheet, stacking them up as you go. Use a large round cookie cutter to cut out 6 circles, then crumple them slightly and lay on top of the casserole dishes.
- Bake the pies for 10 minutes or until the filo is golden and crisp. Dust with icing sugar and serve immediately.

Lemon, Raspberry and Pistachio Cheesecake

SERVES 8

PREPARATION TIME 4 HOURS 40 MINUTES

CHILLING TIME 4 HOURS

INGREDIENTS

50 g / 1 ¾ oz / ¼ cup butter
200 g / 7 oz / ¾ cup digestive biscuits, crushed
50 g / 1 ¾ oz / ½ cup pistachio nuts, chopped
150 g / 5 ½ oz / ⅔ cup cream cheese, well chilled
150 g / 5 ½ oz / ⅔ cup condensed milk, well chilled
2 lemons, juiced

FOR THE TOPPING

100 g / 1 ¾ oz / ½ cup raspberry jelly (jello) cubes
50 g / 1 ¾ oz / ½ cup pistachio nuts, chopped

METHOD

- Melt the butter and stir in the crushed biscuits and chopped pistachio nuts, then tip the mixture into a 23 cm (9 in) round spring-form cake tin and press down firmly into an even layer.
- Beat the cream cheese with an electric whisk until smooth then whisk in the condensed milk. Whisk in the lemon juice until the mixture starts to thicken, then pour it onto the biscuit base and level the top. Chill in the fridge for 3 hours.
- Make up the jelly according to the packet instructions, using only half the recommended amount of water. Leave the jelly to cool a little, then flood the top of the cheesecake with it before it starts to set.
- Return the cheesecake to the fridge for 1 hour. Un-mould the cheesecake and transfer it to a serving plate, then sprinkle with the chopped pistachios.

INDEX